PRAISE FOR *ROAD TO A MIRACLE*

"Shaw's story, told with immense passion, is one to grip his reader as they accompany him on a journey filled with surprising twist and turns, to a final, unexpected ending, overflowing with joy and great blessings."

— Dr. Paul Pearson, director, Thomas Merton Center

"This story will fascinate you and bring you joy. An intriguing tale with a marvelous ending."

— Hall of Fame golf course designer Pete Dye
and his wife Alice

"Shaw's book is compelling. I felt like he was speaking with me directly as he draws us into the ups and downs of his fascinating life journey."

— Dr. Lewis Rambo, author and professor emeritus,
San Francisco Theological Seminary

"*Road to a Miracle* is truly a miracle! What a great read. I could not put it down!"

— David Brofsky, ESPN senior producer

"*Road to a Miracle* is more than Shaw's own story. It's the "duobiography" of himself and of the divine presence guiding him toward the stunning surprise of a miracle."

— Rev. Jim Burklo, author of *Open Christianity*
and *Birdlike and Barnless*

READER COMMENTS

"What a beautiful story! I finished the book on my plane ride from DC to Denver just now. I was blubbering through the last several pages—wiping tears and wiping my nose covertly on my sleeve!"
                                        – Becky Miller, Denver, Colorado

"I cannot count the times when a lump has arisen in my throat while I have been reading this masterpiece."
                                        – Scott Montross, Indianapolis, Indiana

"I love the Miracle book. It really is a miracle. Stories like these tug at our heartstrings, and remind us that, in God's good time, many tangled webs are unraveled and light shines in."
                                        – Rosemary Yokai, Minneapolis, Minnesota

"[Mark Shaw] has always seemed so filled with gratitude and love and light no matter what. I do believe the universe works in mysterious ways . . . "
                                        – Koren Reyes, New York City

"I started crying on page 172 and then cried the rest of the way through the book. I was certainly cheering on the main character! It did feel like reading a Forrest Gump-type story."
                                        – Betsy Blankenbaker, Indianapolis, Indiana

"What a terrific story with a fabulous 'ending' — which is actually the beginning!"
                                        – Tom Yoder, Snowmass Village, Colorado

ROAD
TO A
MIRACLE

MARK SHAW

People's Press
Woody Creek, Colorado

Road To A Miracle
by Mark Shaw

© 2011 Mark Shaw

People's Press
Minds Wide Open

Published by People's Press
Post Office Box 70 • Woody Creek, Colorado 81656
www.PeoplesPress.org

Distributed by Globe Pequot Press
www.globepequot.com

Library of Congress Control Number: 2011928688

ISBN: 978-1-936905-00-3

Cover and Interior Design: Nick Zelinger, NZ Graphics

First Edition
Printed in the United States of America

Dedicated to
Wen-ying Lu, Marni, Allison and Lucy
I love you

and to
James
Thank you for the gift of a lifetime

"*Who is the happier man, he who has braved the storm of life, or he who has stayed securely on the shore, and merely existed?*"
— Dr. Hunter S. Thompson

FOREWORD

I don't believe in miracles. Or magic. I don't believe in god. I am an atheist. Which is an awkwardly provocative and nearly meaningless word that pretty much just describes me as not being a person who believes in anything supernatural. Like luck or fate or karma. As if there should be a special noun for people who don't like baseball or the taste of pizza. So let's just say that I'm an agnostic. On steroids. And the least likely candidate to be absolutely knocked out by *Road to a Miracle*.

Mark Shaw has been my friend for over thirty years. We met during our salad days in Aspen, Colorado (Mark's was the Caesar with romaine and mine the simple mixed greens.) I had recently defected from Buffalo, New York to Hunter S. Thompson's Rocky Mountains in a determined attempt to slip out of a blue-collared birthright and to explore my already lapsing Catholicism. Mark had already finished law school and a stint on his college golf team—a good Christian man from America's heartland.

New Mexico's Henry Deutschendorf had morphed into Aspen's John Denver and both sides of the Continental Divide were singing about the advantages of a Rocky Mountain high. The sexual revolution was enjoying an Indian summer. Skiing was dangerous and one-night stands were still safe. Aspen was a town without parents. Everyone kept wondering when the grown-ups would materialize.

The idea of ever being a mom or a dad was preposterous. Mark and I had reinvented ourselves into personal versions of Peter Pan, and Aspen was our Never Never Land. Nobody grew up; no one got old. We skipped and tripped from one slippery rock to the next in a steady stream of delightfully entertaining misadventures and escapades.

I can't remember exactly why we both decided to move on from Aspen and all of its delights. It may have simply been fatigue or that kind of low-grade nausea one might get from riding too many roller coasters or eating too much lobster. But I do remember both of us setting out, leaving town heading down the highway—albeit taking different forks in the road. We both ended up in entertainment, sometimes known as "show business" and very often not so entertaining.

I have been told that if I didn't know where I was going it didn't matter what road I was on, and of course we have all heard—endlessly now, it seems—that "the journey is the destination." But few of us have lived out our long and strange trips with more aplomb, perseverance and courage than Mark Shaw. It is hard to overstate just how poignant and exquisitely ironic his odyssey has been. Led by what he gratefully and almost apologetically calls a Holy Spirit, Mark has been fearless in following his heart. Finally, arriving at the exact place he had always wanted to be . . . no less astonished as to how he finally got there than the rest of us.

Patrick Hasburgh
Author, *Aspen Pulp*

PROLOGUE

"We will not be communicating with you anymore."

As snow fell at a consistent pace outside my Aspen, Colorado apartment during a freezing winter day in 2004, each word impacted my brain like a thunderbolt. Tears began to well up in my eyes as I read the e-mail message again. Could this be true, I wondered? Were the four stepchildren whom I loved more than anything in the world really telling me they wanted nothing more to do with me, that I would never hear from them again? Was this e-mail message to be the end of a special relationship begun nearly thirteen years earlier when I accepted the responsibility of caring for them as a parent by marrying their mother?

As I sat in complete disbelief, I could not stop crying. Nearby, my beloved canine friend, Black Sox, rose from his slumber and nestled his head against my legs. He could tell that pain had gripped me like a grizzly-bear hug, that something terrible had happened causing me tremendous grief and heartbreak. Then he wandered over and gently placed his wet nose on my elbow, a true sign of loving friendship.

After giving him a quick rub behind the ears, his favorite form of affection, I glanced again at the eight words while trying to understand this harsh dismissal.

Immediately, there was the "poor me" reaction to stepson Kyle's e-mail as my hands grasped my head in anger. How dare they do this to me, I thought, after what I had done for them? I recalled the day when, while in California, I had learned of Kyle nearly breaking his neck in a front yard motorbike accident when he misjudged a jump we had set up on our mini-racecourse. I had rushed back to Indiana to his bedside, showing the love of a father even though I'm not his real dad. When it came to Kevin, one of Kyle's triplet brothers, I remembered how he had broken his leg after making the high school basketball team his senior year. He wanted to rejoin the team for the state tournament and as the leg mended, I rebounded shot after shot so he could round his game into shape. I recalled special times with Kent: the day I taught him how to tie a tie for the first time. And racing turtles with all three boys—and them laughing when my turtle headed backwards. Finally, I recalled the day I surprised my stepdaughter Kimberly by agreeing to let her drive our van to a Grateful Dead concert in Michigan when she expected a strict refusal to even attend the concert. What wonderful memories I had of my days and months and years with the four stepchildren: the trips to Colorado, New York City, and Florida; the time we spent at Disneyworld where, despite being claustrophobic, I risked life and limb by taking a terrifying ride on Space Mountain. Now, if I understood the message correctly, the stepkids were saying, through Kyle, that they never wanted to see me, or hear from me, again.

I called my brother Jack and told him about the rejection. He could barely understand me as I poured out my wounded soul. Then I called Scott, one of my best friends, but my sorrow prevented me from making much sense. My chest was heaving so strongly I thought I might be having a heart attack. "God, how could you let this happen?" I screamed.

Despite the twenty-five-degree temperature, I piled on heavy clothes and took a walk with Black Sox along the Roaring Fork River against the backdrop of the snowy mountains toward Independence

Pass. I cussed my wife Chris, the stepkids, God, the world. Then I threw snowballs at trees as if they were my stepchildren. How ungrateful they were, I told myself, how unfair they were. I did not deserve this treatment, to be cast aside after having helped raise the four of them. Kimberly had only been ten years old when I first met her, and the triplets eight. I wondered if they knew that I had married their mother knowing she could not have any more children. This meant that I would never have children of my own, never be a biological father or grandfather. Did they realize the sacrifice? Did they realize what I had given up?

As the day progressed, I could not figure out how to respond to Kyle's shocking message. Should I explain my heartfelt feelings to him in an e-mail? Or just let it go? For nothing I wrote would, in all likelihood, make any difference. When I finally calmed down, when I was finally done with my pity-party, the realization hit home, the realization that I should have expected my stepchildren's dismissal since in truth there was only one person responsible for my downfall from grace with these kids: me. Kyle knew, and I knew, that the source of his discontent was the messy divorce his mother and I were going through. One day, I had been on top of the world with a happy, loving stepfamily, a successful career as an author and television personality, many special friends and financial security. The next day, or so it seemed, I had been scorned as an "evil stepfather" by a national celebrity—a legendary basketball coach—triggering the loss of my family, of my professional reputation, of any financial stability, and the loss of longtime so-called friends.

How had this happened? How had I reached the low point of a confusing, disorienting two years that had turned my world upside down? Despite denial on my part in what I called "the Knightmare," a full-court war of words with legendary Indiana University basketball coach Bobby Knight, there was no question that my actions had caused my tumble from fame, fortune, and any sense of peace. I was now alone and hurting from Kyle's message. Sitting on a couch with Black Sox at my feet, I began to mentally rewind the mind-boggling events that had led me to this sorry state of affairs. Nothing made sense, and nothing would until sometime later when I realized that the pain and suffering I had experienced since my marriage had broken up was only one piece of the puzzle in a plan a mystical Spirit had in mind for me. This was a plan filled with lessons concerning, among other things, unconditional love, unselfishness, understanding, and most importantly forgiveness, all connected to what I would call Christlike conduct. Out of this misery was to come the greatest teaching moments of my life, and preparation for a miracle masterminded by the magical workings of this Spirit, workings that would permit me to realize a dream, a special gift I could never have imagined possible before.

BOOK I

CHAPTER ONE

The Free Spirit

There was no disputing that as the year 2000 began, I was truly a most blessed man. In other words, I had it made. From birth through age fifty-five, the hard-to-believe streak of special experiences had led me in directions I could never have imagined.

Looking back, I realize that my journey had actually begun in Auburn, Indiana (best known for classic cars like the Auburn Cord-Duisenberg), a small town in the northeastern part of the state. I was born in 1945, the same year President Franklin D. Roosevelt died, Adolph Hitler committed suicide, the United States dropped atomic bombs in Japan, and World War II ended.

Marvin and Vera Shaw were patient, loving parents who put up with my endless shenanigans. Most times during my early years, Mom would simply shake her head at my rather unusual behavior and say to my father, "Marvin, just wait. Mark will grow out of it."

During my first few years on Earth, our family attended a Methodist Church in Auburn, only to switch allegiance to the Presbyterians when we moved to the other end of town. My parents never provided an explanation for the sudden change in churches and this left me wondering if the God I was supposed to worship was all that important to one's daily life.

At first, I was also a bit confused with the use of the words *God*, the *Holy Spirit*, the *Spirit*, *Higher Power*, and so forth. I asked my mom why there couldn't be just one of these to pray to, but she said they all pretty much meant the same thing and that being what she called a "believer" was something universal. Through the years, I remembered her explanation, and used the words interchangeably. Most notably, Mom said, "Respect those who believe as you do in the Higher Power, but also those who don't." I remembered that, too.

Watching my parents raise me, my two sisters Anne and Debbie, and my elder brother Jack had showed me how I hoped to treat my children when I grew up. I learned from them that a parent's love was never ending, and that it took work, hard work, and most importantly, time. Yes, time was the precious gift my parents gave to us kids, as they were always there for us throughout our childhoods.

Dad worked hard, first as a foreman in a factory and then as a real estate agent, but he was always at home whenever possible, showering us with love and understanding. When I wrecked my first car, a nifty '52 green Chevy, by falling asleep at the wheel, he didn't yell at me but only said, "We can fix the car, but not you. That's all that matters." When I lied to him and took a girl named Cindy, whose mother had a terrible reputation, to the high school prom against his orders, he simply sat me down and told me that he expected me to use good judgment in the future. Instead of screaming at me, he was understanding, and did not punish me, or forbid me to see her. (I was pleased to learn that Cindy later became a physician.)

I established a good work ethic during my early years when I first washed cars at a local Chevrolet dealer, and then sold *TV Guide* magazines door to door. Our family also had a small store called

Shaw's Grocery that was an extension of our home. Anne, Jack and I worked there helping the neighborhood customers. My first dog, a cute little brown Pomeranian, was named Lucky; I had won him at the county fair in a raffle. We also had a parakeet, and Mom felt so bad when she left a window open and he flew away.

Mom was a loving woman who expressed her love every day. I always will remember her presence after each of my high school golf matches. She didn't care if I shot seventy or one hundred; scrambled eggs, bacon and toast awaited me whenever I returned home from a match. In 1961, the year I turned sixteen, mom was a bit startled when Mr. Ford, the high school driver's education teacher, called with the news that the car I was learning in had hit a stone wall surrounding the local YMCA. While attempting to turn left on a side street by the Y, I had crept out too far into the intersection. When I turned the steering wheel, I didn't turn it far enough, and drove right into the short wall. Luckily, I was not going too fast and the damage was minimal. Mr. Ford, who was also my high school golf coach, laughed about the incident later, but had no alternative than to give me a D in Driver's Ed. I'll bet there weren't too many people who had ever received such a low grade for a class like that.

Perhaps as a sign of things to come, that same YMCA gave me a chance to display my acting skills. Every year it staged a "Canteen Blackout." (The "canteen" was in reference to the Y's social area, located in a room below the main floor.) For fun, three or four of my high school friends and I danced to a rock 'n' roll tune wearing pink tutus. Thank goodness a photograph my mom took of that performance disappeared long ago.

I began college at Purdue University in 1963, which was also the year that Martin Luther King, Jr. was arrested during civil rights marches, and President John F. Kennedy was assassinated. Aiming to emulate my brother, I attempted a degree in engineering until I earned a rock-bottom score of 5 out of 100 on a physics exam. When I called my father in tears, he simply called me a "Dumbhead," actually a term of endearment, before saying, "Mark, we knew you would never be an engineer. Switch to something more to your liking." Once again, my dad's reaction was unforgettable; he had raised me to think for myself and had led by good example, the greatest teaching a child can have.

Being one to heed my dad's advice, I made the switch from engineering to economics without hesitation. But the fun part of college interested me more than the classroom, so I spent the next five-and-a-half years (including three years in summer school) drinking, chasing women, riding a Harley Davidson motorcycle, and earning a varsity letter on the golf team. At one point during my fifth year (working construction helped me pay the bills), two Beta Theta Pi fraternity brothers and I rented an apartment in the basement of a small off-campus house. My mom visited, but the musty smell and messy conditions made her proclaim, "I will never visit you again." And she didn't. However, our poor habits didn't stop a few of the Purdue coeds from saying hello. One I dated was best friends with All-American quarterback Mike Phipps' girlfriend. Mike was the second-most famous quarterback I knew at Purdue, the first being Bob Griese, later a Super Bowl champion with the Miami Dolphins.

One weekend, a bunch of us piled into Bob's car and drove to the Kentucky Derby. At the betting window, the clerk recognized Bob and started giving us race tips. We won the first four or five, and our winnings totaled a few hundred dollars. Then the clerk recommended "Banana Joe" in the sixth race. Bob, on our behalf, bet all of our money on this horse. We stood by the rail shouting encouragements as Banana Joe blasted out of the gate, but halfway down the stretch,

Joe suddenly stopped, turned around, and headed for the starting gate. He finished dead last. We teased Bob about that for days, calling him "Banana Joe Griese."

To finance my extended college career, I worked as a bartender and waiter at a restaurant called The Pig and Whistle. Peanut shells covered the floor during our standard after-game celebrations. I learned how to pour beer from the tap even though I wasn't of legal age. To the surprise of many in the future who would consider me a terrible dresser, I actually sold clothes at a campus men's store. One month, I won the contest for selling the most sport coats. I also paid a lot of attention to the lovely coeds who frequented the store. Nobody cared when the other salesmen and I asked for a phone number when the darlings signed the credit card bill.

After failing a calculus course, twice, and risking not graduating, I bribed a professor into giving me a D in exchange for teaching his daughter to play golf. Finally passing calculus allowed me to earn a bachelor of science degree in industrial economics in 1969. Final grade point average: a dismal 2.2 (just above a C average). Mom and Dad could not have been too proud of my performance, yet they recognized my free spirit. No one seemed to understand the origin of my individualistic nature, but I was loved for the person I was, and not for what I was supposed to be—just another one of my parents' lessons, one that would prove valuable in the future, I knew, when I became a parent myself.

Neither my days at Purdue University, nor a summer in Chicago when I frequented the pubs in search of my life purpose, had pointed me in the direction of the church. God was always in my mind, but any sense of organized religion didn't make much sense. Maybe I was too busy having fun without the need for any spiritual foundation.

But unbeknownst to me, whatever Spirit was guiding my life was about to bless me in a special way.

If there was a first time when I noticed something completely inexplicable and illogical, something too strange to understand, and something bigger than life, it occurred during the spring of 1968 when the war in Vietnam was raging, and Robert F. Kennedy announced he would run for president, only to be assassinated months later. While others used false doctors' excuses, shot themselves in the leg or arm, or fled to Canada to avoid being drafted into the military, I somehow flunked a hearing test, twice, and was banned from serving. Even today, I can hear the sergeant's voice screaming at me, "Mr. Shaw, you cannot enlist! You cannot be drafted! Do you understand?" This meant I would avoid being classified 1-A (ready for duty), avoid being drafted, and avoid a trip to Vietnam.

Dad had taught me to be responsible, to accept the duty to serve. Shocked at the sudden turn of events and upset at the rejection, I telephoned him, explaining that the Army must have made a mistake. Being the loving father he was, he screamed "Get the hell out of there!" and I quickly scampered out of the building. When a letter arrived classifying me 4-F (physically unfit to serve), I didn't tell anyone as so many of my friends were headed for military duty. Instead of celebrating, I hid the deferment letter in a metal box and never looked at it again.

Years later, I felt guilty and horrified as I watched young men my age killed in a war that didn't make sense to anyone. I wondered why I had been singled out for rejection when I was ready to serve my country. Why was I so fortunate, I asked myself—but I could find no answers. Somehow, I had been protected from danger, prevented from having to kill, and from experiencing violence in its worst form.

Grateful, I was certain a guardian angel of some sort had protected me from possible harm.

Free to pursue a job when others had to risk their lives, I accepted an offer from a chemical company that sorely needed salespeople. After some training in Michigan, they sent me to Minneapolis/St. Paul in the summer of 1968 where I sat at a desk and sold railroad tank cars full of sulfuric acid to industrial companies around the country. I enjoyed the Twin Cities. People were friendly; they loved the outdoors. Unfortunately, my lackluster performance matched the boring nature of the work, but instead of firing me, the company arranged for a transfer to Chicago. There I finally *was* fired when the powers-that-be learned that I was moonlighting as a bartender at a bar on Rush Street called The Depot. One necessary part of the job was to pay off the Chicago beat cops each week so they wouldn't hassle customers with ID checks. The bar required that either I or two of my co-workers give a brown sack full of cash to the men in blue when they stopped by on a regular basis.

Living in Chicago was spectacular. Days were spent watching bikini-clad girls at Oak Street Beach while frolicking in the sun and attempting to figure out what to do with my life. A friend named Pete provided me the opportunity to earn some good money by selling cute little glass swan vases filled with colored water at state fairs. Women loved them, but I was nearly arrested when a New York state patrolman stopped my car as I was towing a U-Haul full of the swans from a factory on the East Coast to Detroit. When he asked me what I was hauling, and I replied, "Glass swans," he bellowed, "Get out of the car, buster." His thorough search confirmed no contraband was present, and the swans and I proceeded to the Michigan State Fair, where police on horseback chased rioters and toppled our boxes, breaking the swans inside. That ended my stint in the swan business, but the fifteen hundred dollars earned provided the money for a new profession: law.

Exactly why I wanted to be a lawyer still remains a mystery, but like I felt about many future adventures that headed me down a different road, it just seemed like the right thing to do at the time. Indiana University Law School in Indianapolis had a well-respected night division, and when the school introduced its day division, it seemed clear that they were looking for bodies whether or not there was a brain attached, which was perfect for me because my marks on the LSAT were mediocre at best. The day I received my admission notice was a grand day all around, another true defining moment of many to follow.

In the fall of 1969, as Richard Nixon attempted to rule the country, the sad news had reached me that my mother was ill. She had been diagnosed with breast cancer. Joining other members of the family, we all attempted to reassure her that recovery was imminent, but the reality was just the opposite during those primitive days of breast cancer treatment. Realizing my mother was going to pass away made me cry for days on end. She was so young, and even though she was sick, her spirit was high and she never wanted pity. When I learned of my acceptance to law school, I raced to her side at the hospital to tell her the news. Mom was in a coma, but as I sat on her bed and told her I was going to be a lawyer, I was certain she heard me.

No woman on Earth ever showed more love to a child than she had shown to me, and if I inherited anything from her, it was compassion for the underdog; she had always told me to treat people the right way, with respect, no matter their plight in life. Mom was a true saint, one of those countless moms nobody ever hears about who simply loves her children, comforts them, and guides their future path with wisdom and a caring way that is difficult to describe. For weeks after Mom died at the young age of fifty-two, I thought of her and how much she loved me. I missed her so much, and swore that if given the chance I would be the same type of father that she had been as a mother. I had learned so much from her, and I dedicated my later years practicing law to her memory.

To be certain, mothers never leave our thoughts no matter how many years pass by. Whenever I smell the aroma of fresh-baked cinnamon rolls, I recall how Mom fixed them for us on cold Indiana mornings. They were plump and tasty and the whole house smelled like a favorite bakery. Mom was also the best at baking chocolate cakes smothered with caramel icing, especially when eaten with a cold glass of milk.

Mom also debunked a few childhood misconceptions that were on my mind. These included the fact that alligators would not eat my toes if my feet stretched over the side of the bed, and (I think my brother Jack told me this one), that I had to hold my hands over my ears when I took a shower because if I didn't, water would flood my brain and I would blow up.

Whenever I hear someone order liver and onions, I always remember Mom trying to get us kids to eat liver. We had it so often that a few times I tucked a piece or two in my socks so I could later feed it to our dog. One time, Mom discovered a pack of cigarettes in my pants before she washed them. She was calm but assertive, telling me that I was using poor judgment to even think about smoking. I never touched a cigarette from that day forward.

Perhaps it was Mom's death that inspired me to seek some spiritual leanings. A huge Presbyterian church on the north side of

Indianapolis captured my attention, and I attended for a short time. But attention to a Holy Spirit looking for me didn't stick as I still felt I could handle the religious part of my life on my own. Did I pray? I'm sure I did, but it was surface prayer asking for too many selfish things as my youthful independence dismissed any need for spiritual connection in my life. My friend and fellow student, Scott Montross, was a good role model as he not only worked part time during the day while attending classes, but was a terrific father as well. I noticed how he balanced his time between work, study and family. Later, his son Eric was the starting center on North Carolina's NCAA championship basketball team and played several years in the NBA. Scott and Janice's daughter Christine went on to not only become a well-established author, but a doctor as well.

Studying hard in law school was new to me, but I accomplished it despite watching my roommate's superb play on the Indiana Pacers basketball team. Billy Keller had been a fraternity brother at Purdue, and we found a $250 a month apartment near the Indiana State Fairgrounds where the team played its games. Despite being merely five feet ten, Billy was a dynamite player, one who especially inspired young kids through his hustling style of play. In one game, he hit nine three-pointers. Wherever we traveled, youngsters flocked around Billy, and I watched dads beaming with pride as they helped their sons get an autograph.

When spring came after the 1969/'70 Pacers season, I met Pete and Alice Dye, the famed golf course architects. My entry into the Dye world began when a friend named Wayne Timberman invited me to play with them at Crooked Stick Golf Course, one of Pete's first designs. Wayne and I had enjoyed some lively times together including playing "hockey" with a couple of female friends on his kitchen floor using golf clubs and ice cubes.

On the first tee, the Dyes suggested we play for a quarter. I thought to myself, "Hey, I can beat a guy wearing work boots and an old golf shirt with dirt smudged on it. And I can certainly beat a woman who looks more like a kindly mother than a good golfer." Accepting the challenge, I walloped a three-hundred-yard drive down the middle. Pete turned to me and said, "Hey, you must not be able to chip and putt or I would have heard of you." Moments later, Alice knocked her second shot into the hole for an eagle, and I never won a hole from her! The Dyes would become great friends over the years, a true blessing.

Playing golf was a weekend luxury since I was wrestling with courses in such evil topics as estate tax, income tax, and property law. But I worked hard and earned a Juris Doctor degree with acceptable grades. I soon overcame the next challenge of passing the bar exam (everyone passed in those days), and became a real lawyer in 1972, when Richard Nixon was reelected president, Alabama governor George Wallace was shot, and the infamous Watergate burglary occurred that would ultimately topple a disgraced Nixon from power.

Instead of jumping into my new profession with gusto, a cute blond named Cindy captured my attention and one evening, while drinking a couple of cold ones, we decided on the spot to flee to Europe. The journey started in Heidelberg, Germany among beautiful fifteenth-century castles, where I intended to learn German and teach at the university. But my prowess to learn the language matched my abilities on that first physics exam at Purdue. Disappointed, but not discouraged, Cindy and I enjoyed the mountains of beer at Oktoberfest and boat rides along the Rhine. We then escaped to Rome where Cindy decided I was not the man of her dreams. She returned to the United States and I was left flat broke with a beat-up, red Volkswagen that nobody wanted. While boarding a train for Luxembourg, I stood on the rail-car steps and heaved the VW keys to a group of Italian men while trying to explain in broken Italian, "Free car. Car free. Car free." Indicative of their generosity throughout my life, my brother Jack and his wife, Sue, saved the day by sending money for a one-way ticket home.

The experience in Europe was a thrill ride for a small-town fellow abroad for the first time. In between eating toasted ham and cheese sandwiches, and drinking the warm beer, I watched German fathers and their sons and daughters together. The fathers appeared quite stern, and perhaps this is why I noted that the children were more respectful towards them. I liked that, and tucked it away in my memory bank. I recognized the importance of respect, a lesson also learned from my parents.

With the dawn of a new career in law approaching, I gave minimal thought as to how these early adult experiences might weave into what was in store for me down the line. Escaping from my small town had provided freedom, but I was still a wandering youth of sorts attempting to figure out life. Later, there would be hardly any question in my mind that what I had experienced was meant to be: dismissal from the military, lessons learned living in the Minneapolis/St. Paul area and Chicago, understanding of the legal system through law school, and exposure to European culture during the trip to Germany and Italy. By age twenty-seven, it was apparent that I was open to any and all new experiences, but little did I know that my adventures had only begun.

CHAPTER TWO

Defending Crooks

After returning to Indianapolis from Europe in 1973, I reconnected with my friend Larry Wallace, a public defender (PD) whom I had interned for when I was a law student.

Larry had to give up his post, however, when he became a state legislator, and hence, one day I was unemployed, and the next I was standing in court as a PD defending James Jethroe, a man in his mid-thirties charged with shooting his girlfriend with a twelve-gauge shotgun from six feet away in front of her three kids. His defense: "I just wanted to scare her by shooting over her head." Despite my loquacious arguments, the jury, after deliberating for about *ten minutes*, convicted Jethroe and sentenced the deserving fellow to life in prison. Regardless, James shook my hand and thanked me for my effort, and bang, I had been christened under fire with the realization that I might make a decent attorney if I worked at it. Three older lawyers named Owen Mullin (the finest trial lawyer I ever knew; his imagination in the courtroom legendary), John "Kit" Carson, and P. K. Ward, took me under their wings and made sure I followed orders when I began to represent private clients as well. Their advice: quit reading law books; practicing law has nothing to do with knowing the law. They were right. Like them, I became a "seat-of-the-pants" lawyer by learning to meander through the court system using my street smarts as a guidepost.

From a secretary named Judy, I learned how tough it was for a single mother to cope with two small children. Another type of unsung heroine we never hear about, she dedicated her every spare moment to Dave and Doug. Watching closely, I noticed how she influenced their early lives, based on her keen observation that kids soak up everything their parents do, their actions, their thoughts, how they treat people, how they act and what they say. I saw firsthand how Judy's kids came first, and the immense responsibility she undertook raising them alone.

After practicing law for nearly a year in Indianapolis, my father visited but could not understand my defending the most dastardly of crooks. One day he accompanied me as I walked to the courthouse with two rough-looking drug dealers, each capable of ripping my throat to pieces if they were so inclined. I assured him they would never kill their lawyer but I don't know if he believed me.

After Mother had died, Dad married a woman with five children. When I was with his new family, I noted how he treated the kids as if they were his own even though he was their stepfather. This didn't stop him from loving them, from being there for those kids, for supporting them as they grew up. Dad was truly a role model for me; he was a strong man with superb character.

Although I had no experience when I began my days as a criminal defense lawyer, cases came my way with ease since I had a reputation of going to the mat for my clients, and doing the extra work necessary to make certain they received a proper defense. My daily regimen consisted of: 6:00 a.m. visits to the county jail to meet with the scoundrels I represented; morning and afternoon court sessions either appearing for clients or defending them in jury trials; and evenings investigating cases before hitting the local taverns for a respite from the immense responsibility of preserving someone else's freedom. Most cases involved trying to help wayward folks avoid responsibility for illegal acts they had committed, including: the defense of a three-time loser charged with stealing French fries from McDonald's; the acquittal of a sexy country western singer named Wanda charged with hiring two thugs to kill her husband (somehow she passed a lie detector test causing me to never trust those results again); working out a deal so the son of famous wrestler Dick the Bruiser could join the Marine Corps instead of going to prison; and an aggravated assault case where my opposing attorney was an assistant prosecutor named Donald Duck. One may only imagine the snickers when I rose to say, "Ladies and gentleman of the jury, can you really believe Mr. Duck?" Someone should have shot his parents for their name choice.

One highly publicized case made me not only feel like the dumbest person in the world, but also the most embarrassed. When an African-American fellow named Ricky shot a white policeman, a manhunt began like none before in Indianapolis. Ricky's mother retained me, and she, the police chief and I appeared on television where his mother, tears rolling down her face, begged her son to turn himself in before a trigger-happy policeman, bent on revenge, killed him.

To make it easy for Ricky to surrender, the police chief suggested that he and I appear on a street corner in a rather crime-ridden neighborhood at 9:00 p.m. The chief said he would be unarmed and no police would try to harm Ricky. True to this promise, the chief and I stood on that street corner, but while we waited, we agreed that this was just about the dumbest thing either one of us had ever done since anyone, including Ricky, considered armed and dangerous, might decide to shoot us both.

As it neared nine o'clock and we were ready to jump in his patrol car and leave, any possibility that Ricky would show was blunted when fire truck sirens wailed in the background. If he was in the area, he must have thought the entire police force was closing in. A few weeks later he was captured in Ohio. When Ricky returned, and was charged with first-degree murder that carried the death penalty, I represented him despite advice from other lawyers that I would be criticized for defending a cop killer. Some nasty threats were made against me, but Ricky deserved representation like any other person charged with a crime. Later, in a packed courtroom, while I was making a passionate argument on his behalf, he stood up, addressed the judge, and screamed, "I don't want Mr. Shaw to be my lawyer. I want to fire him." Embarrassed by the sudden turn of events, I crept out the side door of the courtroom hoping nobody would see me. Ricky's mother was upset, but he wouldn't listen to her when she told him he had made a mistake. With another lawyer by his side, he received the death penalty. Even though I never learned why Ricky fired me, I always felt that I somehow let him down. Years later, I heard he had been stabbed while in prison.

Most people think that defense attorneys and their adversaries, prosecutors and police, are enemies in and out of the courtroom, but that's simply not true. I hosted a friendly dice game in my law office every other week or so. We used a round, wooden, brown table so often that the paint disappeared from the middle. Defense lawyers, prosecutors, police, and even a judge or two stopped by to see if they could win a few bucks. My specialty was hitting 6s, or "sixers" as I called them. After rolling the dice, I'd yell, "Sixer, sixer, sixer, c'mon sixer" as the dice hit a thick law book braced against another book or two. By eight or nine o'clock, there was nonstop action.

The camaraderie was good for everyone, and once in a while, plea bargains for avoiding trials were quietly discussed in a corner or in the hall. Regularly, we placed friendly wagers on football, basketball, and baseball games. Nobody took things too seriously. People might have wondered about whether there were conflicts of interest, or whether adversaries should be socializing, but the basic fact was that when all of us stepped into the courtroom, we showed respect for the opponent while fighting like hell for our clients, or in the case of the prosecutors, for the state. When we walked out of the courtroom, there was no cause for concern that we occasionally gambled a bit or enjoyed a beer or two. During my years as a defense lawyer, some of my best friends were homicide detectives. I had a job to do, and they had a job to do. Some would even refer cases to me when those arrested needed good, sound legal advice, which I greatly appreciated.

During one particular case, justice certainly prevailed although it wasn't the kind people regularly hear about. I defended Harriett, a mild-mannered, African-American woman who had killed her husband by shooting him *five times* in his back in front of a packed courtroom with a pistol she carried for thirty blocks in freezing weather. Harriet was headed straight for prison until I learned that her husband Walter had stomped her seventy-five-year-old father to death in a drunken rage the night before her courtroom escapade. Behind the scenes, I convinced the prosecutor of Harriet's "sudden impulse" to drill Walter based on her sufficient motive to kill him.

Months later, Harriet was granted probation. Vigilante justice had prevailed. Made sense to me.

While celebrating this victory with a bottle of Boone's Farm Strawberry Wine (my favorite), someone called my home identifying himself as F. Lee Bailey, famous at the time because of the Boston Strangler and Patti Hearst cases. I thought it was a friend of mine having fun, and hung up. By the second call, the man said, "This *is* F. Lee Bailey and if you hang up it will be the dumbest thing you ever do." Fortunately, I listened and Lee, who had contacted me based on the recommendation of a local judge, quickly requested that I accept an offer to be co-counsel with him during the representation of a seedy doctor in a city near Indianapolis. The doctor had been charged with "surgically removing" the head of an undercover DEA agent who suspected the doctor of drug trafficking, and then tying the headless torso to a cement block that bobbed up in a farmer's pond one sunny day.

After speaking to the doctor, we arranged for him to visit my offices on a Saturday morning. While checking some trial notes, I looked up from my desk to see the doctor and a woman whom I believed to be his wife, standing at the entryway with their shoes in hand. Before I could speak, he put a finger to his mouth and whispered, "Shhh. Our shoes are bugged." I didn't reply, but nodded toward a small, checkered couch in the corner of the office. There the three of us sat with me in between the two of them. While still whispering, the beady-eyed physician presented me with some questions about his case that he had written on the back of a grocery receipt. After answering them, I walked to my desk while telling him not to keep the paper on him since the police could confiscate his notes and use them against him in court. I leaned down to get a business card, and when I looked up, the doctor had a big bulge in his right cheek. To my bewilderment, he had *eaten the notes*. I didn't react, but afterwards referred to the dandy couple as Dr. and Mrs. Strange. The prosecution could not convict my client of the murder charge, but, in a bizarre twist to the case, they proved at trial he had at one point hired two thugs to blow up his hometown hardware store when the owner overcharged him for lead used in his X-ray machine. The doctor was sent to prison for seven years, but afterwards, because of a loophole in the law, he resumed practicing medicine in Mississippi. Scary.

Watching Lee Bailey in action taught me some good courtroom strategy, but he wasn't at his best. Losing the Patti Hearst case devastated his ego, and he was never the same again.

Despite a good reputation as a defense lawyer for the poor and downtrodden with headline-making cases that kept me in the limelight, I became disillusioned with my new profession after a young fellow charged with theft left my office and, upon exiting, stole my secretary Kathy's purse. While racing after him down a main street in Indianapolis like some sort of Keystone Kop, a thought occurred to me: "Hey, maybe it's time for a change."

While questioning whether a profession as a criminal defense lawyer suited me, I learned of a most disturbing case. A young man had been charged with kidnapping a pretty young woman and driving around with her tied up in his car trunk. After a court hearing where I attempted to lower the man's bond, the kidnapped woman's mother spit in my face while screaming at me for being a worthless derelict. Friends wondered how I could defend someone "I knew was guilty," but as I pointed out to them, only a judge or jury can make that determination, the rationalization every defense lawyer uses at one time or another. When a young lawyer once confessed he thought his client might be guilty, I told him to quit the profession because he did not understand his responsibility. Any good defense lawyer is required to do one thing, and one thing only: protect his or her client's constitutional rights.

The young kidnapper in trouble was the latest in a long line of kids I represented who had gone astray. When I stood in front of a judge with one such youngster, no more than fifteen or sixteen, who had been transferred to adult court because of the severity of his crime, the youngster actually said "thank you" when the judge imposed a heavy sentence. This kid was so naïve, so oblivious to what was occurring that it startled me, made me realize that this child, one with no mother or father to guide his path, was headed to prison where older inmates would tear him apart. Time and time again, I saw that with each senseless crime, lives were destroyed; everyone lost—the victims, of course—but also the ones inflicting the harm. For all practical purposes, once juvenile delinquents entered the prison system, they were goners, especially considering the penal system's de-emphasis on rehabilitation. Many times I sat alone on a courtroom bench or at a tavern and simply shook my head. Parenting was the real problem. The majority of the kids I represented had never been parented, especially by fathers who had either abandoned them or were in prison themselves. Without a father, the kids were lost, and most quit school and drifted into the crime world.

My confusion intensified after I won an acquittal for a sixteen-year-old charged with the senseless murder of a young, innocent social worker. During this trial, the prosecutor made a strong case. My goal was to force the jury to consider everything but the evidence against my client. But I crossed the line by violating my personal ethical standards when I hoodwinked jurors into believing the murder weapon, never discovered, was actually in my suit coat pocket when in truth I had put another gun there to aid my ruse. When we listened to deliberations in a bathroom adjacent to the jury room (permitted in those days), it was apparent that the jurors were confused by my antics when they voted for an acquittal. This was not justice, I knew, but more of a game I was playing, a very dangerous game. I spent many sleepless nights wondering just who I had become, what I had become.

After the jury acquitted the young man, a newspaper reporter named Carolyn walked up to me at the counsel table and said, "What do you think of the verdict?" I looked at her and replied, "That's it. I quit. I'm done. Enough of this. I'm headed for Colorado." She told me she would print the news in the Sunday paper and she did. Shock waves hit the legal community, but I knew if I continued on I would become like many other defense lawyers—a drunk, a drug addict, or a mental patient; the stress involved with defending the lowlifes of society takes a great toll on the soul. Nothing beats the courtroom for drama, but one must constantly be dealing with people from the seedy world of crime who are destroying their lives and the lives of others. It was not for me. I knew that while I could try to limit the damage to young people charged with crimes, the real culprits were the parents—plain and simple.

During my years as a defense counsel, relationships might have permitted the chance to marry and have children. But my restless nature—one continually pressing me toward trying new things—coupled by the responsibility of defending people in trouble, left no time for starting a family. Instead, I enjoyed other people's kids, enjoyed the times I could spend with them at Little League games, the state fair, or visits to the park where I watched fathers and mothers playing with their children. If I ever got my life in order, I thought, I will be one of those fathers.

Within weeks of my "retirement" announcement, I had cleared my basement of Boone's Farm bottles, sold any furniture that wasn't in disrepair, and sold my house to my buddy Billy Keller. Triggered by the love of Colorado during a summer visit there a year or so earlier, I packed my bags for a move to Aspen in 1977, a time when the world was focused on Jimmy Carter's presidency and entertained by such classic motion pictures as *Annie Hall*, *Rocky*, and *Star Wars*.

The cross-country trip I took to Aspen was quite eventful in a strange sort of way. During the previous two years I had accumulated quite a substantial pile of cash, since no good defense lawyer ever represents a client without having first been paid, most times in full. Otherwise, the client may flee the jurisdiction if he or she feels they will be jailed. Getting the money up front, and in cash, is the first rule of being a top-notch defender, and my more experienced friends initiated me with that knowledge early in my career. Before I left Indiana, I gathered up the cash I had stashed inside old law books stacked on the shelves in my offices. No one bothered to look there, but as time passed, the books got fatter and fatter. By the time I was ready to leave for Colorado, I had a large leather bag filled with tens, twenties, fifties, and hundred-dollar bills. At home, I began stuffing the bills into pockets, socks, extra pairs of shoes, pants, and shirts, anywhere I could hide the cash in my car. All told, I had collected about twenty-five thousand dollars, a considerable amount in those days, which I hid in the clothes, under the seats, in the glove compartment, and in the trunk under the spare tire for my drive west to Colorado.

During the trip, I kept looking in the rearview mirror to see if there was someone following me. My car was a bright red convertible, not exactly easy to miss. I never stayed in any hotels; just slept in the car. One day right outside some small Kansas town, my hands started shaking when I saw the swirling red lights of a police car behind me. I pulled over, ready to be locked up forever as a drug dealer or bank robber, but then the police car whizzed by me. I had almost wet my pants I was so nervous. When I crossed over Independence Pass and arrived in Aspen, I threw the money in a grocery sack, found a friendly bank, and used a safe deposit box to keep my savings secure.

Moments after hitting Aspen, another one of those right-place, right-time moments occurred. I stopped at a small café, and before long a stranger sitting in the next booth struck up a conversation with me. His name was Dwight, and I soon learned he was a lawyer looking for a law clerk. Even though my research skills were mediocre at best, which I disclosed, Dwight hired me on the spot. Back then Aspen didn't have much of a law library in the courthouse, so I had to drive to Glenwood Springs, about an hour away, to use its courthouse library. Bored with the research, I spent more time soothing my body in the famous hot springs there than at the courthouse. Dwight became a bit suspicious of how much time I was spending in Glenwood, and with my legal research skills leaving something to be desired, he finally fired me. But it was a "friendly" firing, as in, "You are the worst law clerk I have ever met but I like you anyway," and he and I became good friends over the years.

John Denver, the singer/songwriter of *Rocky Mountain High* along with many other hit songs, lived in Aspen at the time. Since

I had the round wire-rimmed glasses before he did, and our face shapes and hair color matched, *he* looked like *me*. At the urging of friends, I began leveraging the resemblance to impress women until I was forced to sing *Rocky Mountain High* in public. My rendition caused coyotes in the nearby hills to howl.

One snowy afternoon, a friend named Mike introduced me to John while we were skiing on Aspen Mountain. "Hey," Mike roared, "here's someone who gets mistaken for you all the time." Somewhat dubious of the invitation, John nevertheless skied toward us dressed in a fancy blue outfit that must have cost one thousand dollars. After Mike said, "This is Mark Shaw," John grinned that famous million-dollar grin of his and said, "Haven't I seen you in the mirror?" I replied with something stupid and tried to ski away, but my ski pole got in the way and I fell headfirst into a snow bank. John and Mike had a chuckle about that as my face burned red.

At bars, people would ask for my autograph, believing I was John. I told them I was not, but they made me sign their napkins or record albums anyway. The joke was that when they returned home, they would tell family and friends they had met John Denver, but he signed his name "Mark Shaw." John never knew of this, but I heard he was a bit upset at times when my lighthearted friends would walk up to him at a restaurant or bar and say, "Hey, Mark, how ya doin'?" For some reason, he didn't think that was too funny.

Skiing became a passion, even though I remained a "social skier." I would take the ski lift to the Sundeck, an open-air restaurant/bar at the top of Aspen Mountain, drink and carouse all day in the sun, and then ski one run down to The Little Nell, the lively pub at the base of the mountain. While most of the skiers wore multi-colored ski outfits like John Denver's, my standard dress consisted of blue jeans, a checkered work shirt, and a Cubs baseball hat. Very stylish.

Par for the course, I experimented with marijuana, but I was a lightweight. One day, while what police might call "under the influence," I took off the ski pants that a friend had lent me in the middle of Main Street and forgot I wasn't wearing anything underneath. Two naïve tourists from Wichita shrieked before I realized why they were shrieking. The mischievous weed had made me act like a fool. It wasn't the only time.

During one drunk and stoned night in a back room reserved for rowdies at a favorite Italian restaurant called the Motherlode, my friend Mike (he denies this, but it is true) disappeared from our large table and we couldn't find him. When the swinging door to the kitchen opened, we noticed he had passed out near the potato peelings under the sink. Apparently he was so inebriated he fell back in his chair and slid into the kitchen when the door opened.

The rich and famous gathered every day at the infamous Hotel Jerome bar on Main Street. One evening Jack Nicholson sat at a table with a bunch of us. One of his friends kept egging him on, and because he was so drunk or stoned, or both, he reenacted his famous scene from the film *Five Easy Pieces* where he wants to order toast but the waitress doesn't let him because the time for breakfast has passed. He then orders a bacon, lettuce and tomato sandwich, but tells her to hold the bacon, lettuce and tomato. Instant toast! We howled at his performance as that infamous devilish grin of his spread across his face. It was the same grin that had made him famous in *Easy Rider* with Dennis Hopper and Peter Fonda when Nicholson is wearing the football helmet.

Alongside all the Aspen characters, we organized a softball team. Nicholson was supposed to play right field but he never showed up. We did have a crazy local roustabout named John, a centerfielder whose marijuana-induced state had him catching fly balls only if they were hit directly to him. If he could not reach out with his glove and catch the ball, he let it go and never chased it. No wonder we never won a game.

To say Aspen was laid back at the time is an understatement. Folks had fun, and the pace was slow and easy, unlike the days later when the rich and famous took over the town. Tom Yoder, a friend from Purdue, drove an old Volkswagen. He promised his daughter she could watch when the odometer turned to 100,000 miles. While in Aspen (he lived ten miles or so away in Snowmass), he noticed the odometer had hit 99,999. To make sure he didn't disappoint his daughter, he put the Bug in reverse and backed it down the dirt roads to his home.

Despite temptations abounding, I never got into hard drugs like cocaine or heroin, but during one down-valley party I did encounter some marijuana procured from the Far East called "Thai-stick." I had a bad dose of the "munchies" and sauntered into the kitchen. On the table was a freshly baked blueberry pie. I couldn't resist a bite or two, and before I knew it, I had eaten the whole pie. Suddenly, my eyes began to blur up and I felt dazed. When I returned to the living room, and stood against a wall with a big grin on my face, I remember someone asking me what was wrong as I heard Jimmy Hendrix's *Purple Haze* blaring across the room. Then a friend, returning from the kitchen, said to everyone, "Who ate the pie?" Between laughs, I admitted that I had eaten it. "The whole pie?" she asked. "Yes, sorry about that. I just couldn't stop," I replied. I thought she was going to be upset, but instead she started laughing, and announced, "Mark just ate the pie with the hash in it."

Hearing this, I stumbled to a couch stoned out of my mind and it wasn't long before I was singing my bad rendition of *Rocky*

Mountain High at the top of my lungs. Luckily, the heavy dose of hash didn't kill me, but I was stoned for a couple of days. The story made the rounds for months. "Eaten any blueberry pies lately, Mark?" people would tease me.

Later that year, during a party at the trendy, riverside cottage of Don Henley, a member of the band the Eagles, there was a pile of cocaine stacked six inches high and wide. Aspen police officers were among the partygoers, and according to the code of justice in the area, "No one gets arrested unless he or she kills someone in front of at least ten witnesses. Otherwise, anything goes." Hence, few arrests were ever made. This was especially true at the "locals only" restaurant and bar Little Annie's. If there wasn't a fistful of fights during the evening, it was a slow night. Law enforcement, especially Sheriff Bob Braudis, a giant of a man with a good sense of justice, let the locals look out for their own.

My past found its place soon enough in Aspen when *Moon River* crooner Andy Williams' wife Claudine Longet (accidently?) shot famous skier Spider Sabich. F. Lee Bailey's agent, whom I met when Lee worked with me, recommended yours truly to ABC's *Good Morning America* as a legal analyst when Lee, a regular contributor, was busy with a case. My reports from the trial were well received, and then I amazed everyone by securing the only interview Claudine ever gave. She sat on the side of a mountain near town and explained, in that cute French accent of hers, how she had mistakenly fired a small gun resulting in Sabich's death. Found guilty of a lesser offense despite the homicide, she served thirty days in jail.

Good Morning America continued to use me as a roving reporter covering "hard-edged" human-interest stories, including: poker champions "Texas Dolly" Brunson and Amarillo Slim in Las Vegas; ugly dog contests in Northern California; Texas armadillo races in

Luckenbach, Texas where Willie Nelson hung out; the Calaveras County Frog Jumping Contest; and the world wrist-wrestling championships in Petaluma, California. These events occurred after I had reluctantly agreed, despite having claustrophobia and vertigo, to join a crack Air Force pilot in an F-4 fighter jet so as to report on the excitement of war games at Nellis Air Force Base in Nevada. I had first refused this assignment, but my agent told me that if I did, the program might not hire me in the future. With much reservation, I climbed up the jet ladder and deposited myself in a sealed cubbyhole behind the pilot. As we taxied down the runway, he asked me, "Listen, do you just want a joy ride, or the whole ball of wax?" Not wanting to seem like a wimp, I said, "Let her rip" or something dumb like that. Seconds after he inverted the plane with the skyline of Las Vegas in the background, I threw up all over my brand new Air Force uniform. Vomit eked into his cockpit and onto his uniform. A small camera captured the mess and *Good Morning America's* hosts laughed, and laughed some more, as they played the tape over and over during the next few days.

True to his word, the agent was right, and my taking the risk caused the program to hire me as a part-time correspondent in place of Geraldo Rivera, who moved into the ABC news department. One of the assignments was to stand next to a special Marine unit and a copy of the Declaration of Independence in Washington, DC on the Fourth of July. Rivera, still with the program on a part-time basis, was at the Statue of Liberty, and co-host Sandy Hill was stationed somewhere in Kansas where a gala parade would take place later in the day. When co-host David Hartman called my name, and the red light on the camera in front of me illuminated, I was supposed to talk about the sacred document, but I completely froze and could not say a word. The Marines remained quiet while I forgot my lines.

I mumbled something about my microphone not working as an excuse, but the powers-that-be at *Good Morning America* were not happy with me at all.

The next time I traveled to New York City, the executive producer gave me the evil eye. That evening, to soothe my wounded soul, a program producer asked me if I would like to visit a new spa called Plato's Retreat. I jumped at the chance, but the night turned sour when the producer and I walked in only to discover his wife frolicking in a Jacuzzi naked with a local television personality. The surprised look on her face, and the shock on his, had me believe the marriage was doomed.

During that New York trip, another *GMA* producer told me that the program was considering hiring model Cheryl Tiegs for a special segment on fashion. He asked if I could interview her on camera to see how she could handle a Q&A. I jumped at the chance, but when we began the interview, it was difficult to think of questions since she was so unbelievably, fabulously sexy and beautiful. Her greenish-blue eyes flashed like diamonds, and I fell in love with her instantly. The gibberish that I spouted didn't make much sense, but she must have understood something since the show hired her on the spot. When she walked away from the set, I followed her like a little puppy dog thinking, "Please take me home; please take me home." I'm pretty sure she could tell I was smitten by the drool wetting the edges of my mouth.

When *GMA* asked if I could interview the illustrious gonzo journalist Hunter S. Thompson, author of *Fear and Loathing in Las Vegas*, I managed to persuade Hunter to meet me at the Jerome Bar at ten o'clock one evening. A film crew had flown in from New York City and I arrived a little before nine to prepare. Ten o'clock came and went. Then 11:00 p.m. Then midnight. Finally, at 4:00 a.m., we all gave up and staggered out of the bar and caught some sleep. The next day Hunter, the ever-present cigarette in a holder dangling from his mouth, ambled by me on Main Street in what appeared to be a drug-induced stupor. I said, "Hey, Hunter, we missed the interview last night," but he just glared at me like he had no idea one had been scheduled, or who I was. In fact, he could barely tell who he was. This was the same man who had nearly been elected county sheriff years earlier. Years later, I attended one of his book signings and chatted with him for a few minutes as he signed the book *Hey Rube*. Believe me when I say that Hunter, arguably one of the greatest journalists who ever lived, made absolutely no sense that night rambling about something incomprehensible.

After failing miserably to land an interview with the Gonzo man, F. Lee Bailey arranged for me to visit Cripple Creek, Colorado, near Pike's Peak. Bailey had been contacted by the famous *Sun Signs* author, Linda Goodman, regarding the disappearance of her daughter. Upon entering her Victorian house, I saw the mystical Linda, her piercing blue eyes staring right through me, sitting in a rocking chair in a dimly lit room surrounded by at least twenty-five purring cats as the aroma of incense filled the air. We chatted as the felines examined me. No luck occurred with finding her daughter, but Linda decided to include me in her book *Love Signs* in a section where she described the relationship between Pisces men and women. In view of later events in my life, Linda pegged me correctly. She said I was a wanderer whose restless nature would educe all sorts of mystical experiences. When my miracle occurred many years later, I recalled how Linda had presaged all that had happened. She was a true mystic with an authentic spiritual aura about her.

One story I covered for *Good Morning America* made me shiver afterwards. To investigate how the mob was infiltrating Atlantic City, I interviewed the Philadelphia lawyer for gangster Angelo Bruno. When the story aired, producers asked me to interview him again. I called his office, but the secretary, her voice shaking with fear, quickly said, "He's dead. They blew him up in his car last night."

Linda Goodman would have appreciated how one of my *Good Morning America* segments had carried me to the next leg of my ever-winding journey. The program sent me to Miles City, Montana in the early summer of 1978 to interview the owners of the nation's smallest network television station. It was an NBC affiliate and truly a mom-and-pop operation. During the evening news, the mother, a jolly woman in her sixties, used puppets to present the weather report. The father, also sixty or better, wore the baseball hat of the team that had won that day's featured game. The eccentric couple was a hoot, and I really enjoyed watching them have so much fun together.

The morning of the telecast, I ate at a small restaurant near the station. On the table was an eleven-by-fourteen-inch one-sheet copy of the *Miles City Daily News*. The front page presented news in the middle and little boxes featuring advertisements at the edges of the paper. The back page displayed the boxes too, but they surrounded sports, weather and public announcements. Always one to be on the lookout for a good idea, I took the paper back to Aspen and showed it to Dave Danforth and Lee Duncan, new friends of mine who worked at the local radio stations. We decided that such an idea might work in Aspen since there was only *The Aspen Times*, a weekly newspaper.

Using the *Associated Press* wire at Dave's station as our national/international news source, we began to lay out our newspaper by adding local news, local and national sports, local weather, ski conditions, and public announcements. On July 4, 1978, the first issue of the *Aspen Daily News* was born. We sold advertisements for a few bucks and if we didn't sell out the boxes, we invented business names to fill the space. One was John's Hot Stew. People kept asking where it was and Dave or I replied, "You mean you don't know?"

One of our great early stories was about Aspen State Teacher's College. The college didn't actually exist but nevertheless caused parents from around the country to call for admission information. A real character named Al Pendorf had made a bunch of money selling T-shirts and other Aspen State Teacher's College memorabilia from a storefront location.

The paper—with its motto "If you don't want it printed, don't let it happen"—took off, and before long it was four pages, then eight, and then sixteen. Today, the *Daily News* is still alive and well with Dave as the owner.

While our newspaper was blossoming, I still made appearances on *Good Morning America*. Those who knew me were amazed that a small-town yokel with absolutely no television experience had managed to appear on network television. Getting on the small screen was a big deal in those days. Most who aspired for television fame had to start at the bottom, perhaps at a network affiliate, but I had begun at the top.

My relevant "training" consisted of talking to juries and so I pretended the camera was a juror and spoke directly to it. To give me a Rocky Mountain high look, I even purchased a new brown corduroy sport coat since all I owned at the time were the blue and khaki ones I alternated for courtroom appearances. My trademark had been a tan trench coat like the one Peter Falk wore on *Columbo*.

During a flight to Aspen, I had left it on the plane. At the time, it seemed like losing that coat was meant to be, a symbol for my leaving the law profession.

One time during my *Good Morning America* days, I visited the home of friends Dave and Nancy Foley. When I knocked at their door during a return trip to Indiana, their youngest child Tim answered through a screen door. He took one look at me and raced into the other room shouting, "Mommy, Mommy, Mark Shaw just came through the television set!"

Observing the Foleys made me envious of their family life, something missing from mine. Sure, I was as free as the proverbial bird to live where I wanted to, work as I pleased, be unaccountable to anyone, but I had no real roots, no family to call my own. When I sat in the Foleys' living room and watched them interact with their children—Erin, Katie, Sheila, and Tim—I could tell that the kids knew they were dearly loved by two parents who showed their love every day.

When Father's Day rolled around, there was no one to celebrate with as Dad lived several states to the east. I always sent a card or a present and called, but later I was to regret not taking the time to visit him on that special day. Instead, I watched others enjoying the special bond they shared with a son or daughter. I found myself wanting to find someone to share my life with so I might have a child, but then my restless nature would propel me to move on at the slightest temptation.

During this time in Aspen, I was not a regular at church services, and believed that any faith I had in a higher power was a private matter that I could handle on my own. Like others during tough times, I prayed to God, but superficially. I thought that by being what

I called a "good person," I was living according to a standard that made sense. This was enough for me, a rationalization to be certain.

If friends were dumbfounded with the appearances on *GMA*, they were even more astounded with the announcement in 1979 that I was being considered as a co-host for a prime-time CBS program called *People*, named after the popular magazine. Apparently Hollywood legend David Susskind, the creator of the program, the producer of movies and stage plays, and the famous host of a long-running late night interview show, had seen one of my *GMA* reports and liked what he saw. I expected a high-level, rigorous interview when he met with me at a Burbank, California studio. My hands sweaty, I was escorted into his fancy office where television and movie scripts lay on tables, chairs, and a large sofa by the door.

Susskind's deep, gruff voice when he shook my hand and said hello made me uncomfortable. I readied myself for a hardball-type interview, but to my surprise, he took one look and said, "If you don't wear those wire rim glasses and look like John Denver, you are hired."

I agreed, and I was.

BOOK II

CHAPTER THREE

California Dreamin'

To satisfy David Susskind, my glasses disappeared when he was around, and soon a move from Aspen to New York City was in the works. Big city, bright lights, the big-time—I couldn't believe it. The first time I took a walk through Central Park, I kept looking up at the skyscrapers. When I ran over a little kid eating a strawberry ice cream cone, his mother screamed so loud I thought I had killed him.

My *People* co-host was none other than the fabulously beautiful former Miss America, Phyllis George, a sweet woman with a sweet-tooth lust for chocolate cream donuts. The show was a grand idea, but unfortunately, the CBS news department hated the show and Phyllis with her smiley ways. Critical reviews were less than kind toward her. I escaped any wrath since I was truly the second banana. The public never watched *People* anyway since the program was opposite *Monday Night Football*. Others just hated the show because they were looking for more substance then, before all the fluff programs hit television-land. A friend of mine told me later that when our show appeared, it was so bad that he actually turned it off. Our failure was especially tough on the executive producer, a no-nonsense African-American woman who was the first of her race to be executive producer of a prime-time television program.

Regardless, the show was a winner all around for me. During the second week of filming, I experienced a ride in a race car with Paul Newman (yes, he is short, and yes, the blue eyes are mesmerizing) during a practice run for the Watkins Glen road race; nearly threw up during an LA rollercoaster ride with child star Kristy McNichol; and ate hamburgers with connoisseur/actor Robert Morley during the filming of *Who Killed the Great Chefs of Europe?* While interviewing Newman, I had to pinch myself realizing that I was in the presence of one of the most famous movie stars in the world. Who would have ever thought a fellow born in small-town Auburn, Indiana would be sitting in the race car passenger seat next to the star of *Cool Hand Luke*, *The Verdict*, and co-star of *Butch Cassidy and the Sundance Kid*? As I watched him deftly switch gears from my passenger seat viewpoint, my head was spinning. "This is Paul Newman," I kept thinking. Damn!

The chance to meet Newman had kept me awake for several nights. But he was like many other cordial celebrities I met. Unlike the ones who didn't want to trust me to give them a fair shake, the confident ones understood that I had a job to do and they wanted to help. Newman, wearing his spiffy Budweiser uniform, was standing by his race car when I first met him. He shook my hand, handed me a helmet, put on his, and said, "Let's go for a ride." As we whizzed around the race course at top speed, he sensed my discomfort and tried to calm me; he must have suspected my legs were shaking. They were. When the ride was over, Paul (he laughed when I first called him "Mr. Newman") and I toasted a couple of cans of Bud. The few people who watched that segment when it aired must have enjoyed my facial expressions. I looked like a ghost, especially when he roared around a hairpin turn at speeds in excess of ninety miles per hour.

Since I was not allowed to wear my glasses on camera and contacts hurt my eyes, I wore my wire-rims whenever I was off camera. On one occasion, I forgot that I couldn't read the questions I had written on note cards during an interview. But I winged it, using the skills learned when I cross-examined police officers during murder trials. Later, the producer asked me why I had omitted some questions she wanted me to ask. I concocted some kind of excuse because I couldn't tell her that I had interviewed the celebrity half blind.

Low ratings, and I mean low, finally led to the cancellation of *People* after six weeks. Later, any chance Phyllis had to resume her television career ended when she hosted a network morning program and tried to get a convicted rapist recently released from prison, and his victim, to hug. Her heart was in the right place, but once again, the critics killed her.

Living in New York City near the United Nations Building permitted yet another view into parenthood. Despite what people say, East Coast folks are different; they are much less sociable, especially to outsiders. During strolls in Central Park, I never saw much affection shown to kids although I am certain they were cared for. I also noticed that the kids seemed a bit "bratty" to me, less respectful than those in the Midwest or Colorado. Once again I was reminded how children emulated their parents. Nasty parents; nasty kids.

Having *People* cancelled could have dampened my spirits, and I was disappointed for sure, but since appearing in a prime-time program was such an unexpected turn of events, something so many other people never experience, it did not take long for me to regain my positive outlook on life. I enjoyed life in New York City, but I yearned to return to the western part of the country. Like many times in the future, I never wanted to go backwards, and while I loved Aspen, I wanted something new, a fresh experience in an unfamiliar place. When *GMA* co-host Sandy Hill offered to let me live in an unoccupied house she owned in Pacific Palisades, California, a few miles from the Pacific Ocean, I jumped at the chance. Soon, with my few belongings packed into the car, I drove cross-country on a road trip, one of my favorite things to do. Along the way, I tried once again to make sense of the unusual experiences that had come at me from every direction. Why me, I continued to ask? Why me?

At Sandy's house, I slept in the one cushy chair she had. During the days, I drove to nearby Malibu and walked the sandy beaches. Southern California was a sleepy place with a laid-back perspective on life, a far cry from the hustle and bustle of New York City. Watching the dogs play in the surf, I wondered what special blessings were in store for me now. The unexpected had become the expected in my life.

When I tired of living in Sandy's empty house, I moved south to the quaint, seaside village of Corona Del Mar just north of Laguna Beach. There the smell of jasmine brought daily bliss, and I lived in a tiny apartment behind a small cottage where an eighty-year-old angel named Mabel tended to hundreds of hummingbirds in her backyard. She had a light-up smile and a great outlook on life. How I loved to sit and just listen to Mabel talk among the flittering hummingbirds about her family, especially her granddaughter, Joy, whom she cared for dearly.

For fun, I drove around the winding streets of Laguna Beach in an old, purple, beat-up Mercedes. A good friend named Mike Stipher and I drank champagne and sang "My Sherona" at the top of our lungs as we drove around town. These were the carefree times when anyone could simply drive to an airport, park free across from the terminal, walk in carrying any number of bags, purchase a ticket without showing any identification, walk to the gate, get on the airplane, and be on his way. Young people today can't imagine this happening, but it did—no driver's license requirements, no security checks, no baggage limits, nothing. The airlines even served free meals.

Sunshiny days at the beach were commonplace. One friend named Herbie, a lover of any and all beers, startled sunbathers at nearby Manhattan Beach one day when he ran up and down the beach shouting "Shaw for King, Shaw for King" based on his belief that I should rule the world. Two other friends, Sam and Jeff (a.k.a. Coyote, named after Wile E. Coyote, the cartoon character), joined the fun. Jeff had a great idea, posting televisions in airports, but no one thought that made sense then.

All the while, I kept in touch with my father and brought him up to date on my latest adventures. He thought my television work was decent but told me I needed a haircut, and a new outfit or two. I was used to these kinds of comments from him, but I was never much for new clothes and instead enjoyed a steady diet of sport shirts, khaki pants, and sneakers.

Pete Dye, the golf course architect, became my "clothing" mentor. At one point, he asked me to buy him some khakis in California because he couldn't find them in the Midwest. "Get twelve pairs or so," he said. "They will last me for the rest of my life." When he visited Palm Springs to work on the PGA West course he was designing, I drove out to see him. Along with our friend Wayne

Timberman, we tried to hit a golf ball over a pretty steep mountain alongside the course Pete had designed. Of course we couldn't, but we laughed when other players on a nearby green laughed at the effort. Later, I heard the story of how Pete's hotel hot tub kept clogging up. The manager couldn't figure out why until he noticed all of the sand at its bottom. Pete finally admitted that when he returned to the room, he would rush to the tub with his sandy pants to wash them while relaxing in the warm water. The manager finally put an end to that routine by buying Pete a few more pairs of pants and making him swear to take the dirty ones to the hotel laundry.

Pete became a father figure to me. I adored listening to him tell stories, many of which were actually true. He was one of those guys, like another friend, Jack Leer, who laughed while telling stories, always making me laugh, even if the story wasn't very funny.

Whenever I visited my own father in Indiana, I was amazed at how the stepchildren loved him. He had been their saving grace. Father's Day was special to him since the kids called him Dad, which meant a great deal to him, and to me. When I would hear the word "dad" at age thirty-six or so, it made me really think about settling down. But a long-term relationship never became longer, and a chance to settle with a lovely woman turned sour. Whether I was mature enough to be able to handle being a husband complete with fatherhood at that point was debatable, but I did feel alone.

Believing the practice of law and a "real job" was beckoning again, I took a brush-up course in preparation for the California bar exam. My friends and family were as surprised as I that I had earned a passing grade.

Then right before my second attempt at attorneyhood, my agent at the William Morris Agency persuaded the CBS affiliate in San

Francisco that I was the perfect person to be one of three hosts of a new afternoon program. This proved to be a dismal idea all around. During rehearsals, nothing worked and the program was cancelled before it even went on the air. My agent threatened to sue when CBS wouldn't honor the contract, but they eventually paid me. No matter, living in the famous City by the Bay made me fall in love with the area. I promised myself that if I could ever live there full time one day, I would.

During this time, Dad and my stepmother Mona visited. I jumped at the chance to show them around the Bay Area. We spent some special times together, culminating with my taking him to the legendary Pebble Beach golf course near Monterey. Images of the two of us playing that beautiful seaside course have never left my memory. It was the perfect father-and-son moment. Once, when he was standing over a putt with the sparkling waters of the Pacific behind him, I felt as if I were going to cry. Living in California was grand, but Indiana seemed like it was as far away as the moon. I missed my dad, and the rest of my family.

One father I admired was Sandy Alderson, an attorney who became general manager of the Oakland A's baseball team. He and his wife Linda lived above me, and I watched how they raised their two children. From them I learned that discipline worked if it was coupled with love, in order that the kids never question how much they were cared about. More than anything, in Sandy and Linda's life, the kids, Brynn and Katie, came first. Always. This was the same example another couple, Mike and Anne Horii, set with their kids.

Due to their influence, I became a big brother for the first time. John was the son of my hair stylist in South San Francisco. A single mother, she wanted her son to have a male influence in his life. When she asked me to spend time with John, I jumped at the chance. He was ten years old, and I did all the things I had hoped one day to do with a son—we bowled, went to the movies, and attended a San Francisco Giants ballgame. John was a good little fellow with a bright smile. He made me want to find a wife to have a son like him with, but I could not seem to promote any of my several relationships to a long-term commitment.

One Father's Day, John and I went to the beach and I felt like a father even though I wasn't his real father. My heart was swimming with delight as I watched John play in the sand. When he gave me a Father's Day card, I held it close to my heart for days on end.

Months later, saying good-bye to John was a sad day all around as I moved back to Los Angeles. Once again, I hit my head against the wall as I tried to land more television work while masquerading as an entertainment lawyer. I soon joined an established Beverly Hills lawyer at his office just down the street from where the first California Pizza Kitchen restaurant was established. A few lower-level clients, not big stars by any means, hired me to help them. One who surely needed assistance with resurrecting her reputation was Donna Rice, a pretty brown-haired lass and former girlfriend of the Eagles' Don Henley. She became romantically involved with Colorado Senator Gary Hart at the time when he had aspirations of becoming president of the United States. When a photograph of Donna sitting on the good senator's lap on the yacht appropriately named "Monkey Business" taken in the waters off the island of Bimini made the rounds, Hart's presidential hopes died and Donna was made the villain. We met in a tiny French restaurant on Beverly Drive but there was little I could do for her except listen and sympathize since the bad publicity surrounding the affair had tarnished her reputation.

During this time, after reading several novels adapted into screenplays, I thought, what the heck, I can write a novel based on my legal experiences. It was called *Professional Courtesy* and I sent it to a literary agent. To my shock, he called the writing "sophomoric," falling short of established literary standards. I'm sure he was right as it was my first try. To my later regret, I gave up on that book, one of the few times in life rejection made me surrender.

With a law office in Beverly Hills, I had just enough credibility to lure British actor and producer Richard Johnson, once married to film star Kim Novak, to hire me as an attorney for the prestigious film consortium, United British Artists. Its member board included Academy Award winners Maggie Smith (*Room with a View*), Glenda Jackson (*A Touch of Class*), John Hurt (*The Elephant Man*), and Albert Finney (*Erin Brockovich*).

Richard, a dear friend and gifted Shakespearian actor, and I flew to London regularly and met with, among others, Ben Kingsley, the Academy Award-winning star of such films as *Gandhi, Turtle Diary, Bugsy,* and *The House of Sand and Fog.* At an Indian restaurant, I sat and listened to Richard and Ben—just after he played Gandhi—wax on about the acting profession. It felt like I was eating chicken curry with the mystical guru who had used peaceful nonviolence to free India from British rule.

While in London, I watched Richard with his wild group of kids. He was a real swashbuckling character and the children adored him. Perhaps, I thought, this might be the right time to get married and have children. The year was 1984, when President Ronald Reagan celebrated the fortieth anniversary of D-Day. I was just a year shy of forty, the perfect time to settle down. But nothing stuck, and I continued to enjoy other people's kids while noticing how Hollywood types had to cope with all of the temptations children could find in la-la land. Did I really want to be a father in that environment? The answer was no.

Despite disappointments at every turn, my stubborn streak instigated numerous head-banging attempts to land more television work. When the ABC morning affiliate asked me to sub-host *Good Morning LA*, I promptly screwed up by showing the other co-host, Cyndy Garvey, wife of LA Dodgers' first baseman Steve Garvey, a lovely photograph of Steve and the couple's two daughters from the morning *LA Times*. I hadn't realized they had separated and were filing for divorce. Gasps from the technical crew alerted me to the faux pas and I apologized to Cyndy. She took it well, but the show producers did not. Learning of the animosity between the couple made me wonder about the kids. If I ever married, and had children, I would never divorce. Never.

My appearance on another LA morning show with co-host Meredith MacRae of *Petticoat Junction* fame resulted in an interview with Baltimore Orioles pitcher Jim Palmer in his Hanes underwear. He was a poster boy for good looks, and standing in his briefs on the set caused many *oohs* and *ahs*. I had grown up a Chicago Cubs fan, but this was the first time I had met a real big league ballplayer. Like a kid, I had him autograph a baseball before he left. Meredith was smitten with the hunk, but Palmer never looked at her while boosting Hanes, a sponsor of his at the time. In the future, when I watched Palmer pitch on television, all I could think of was him standing on the mound in his white briefs.

During this period, my sister Debbie and her husband Tom lived in nearby Long Beach. When their first son Michael arrived, I drove her and the tiny baby home from the hospital as Tom had to travel for his job. I loved to be around Michael and Debbie. I watched how much love she showed her newborn. I even helped when it was time for him to walk. I held his hands as his little feet tried to make steps on the carpet. When he fell down, we laughed and he looked at us with a curious smile; apparently falling down was as much fun as walking. He also liked when I would touch his nose with the tip of an ice cream cone.

All the while, I communicated every week with my father. Dad was the ultimate giver, and he continued to treat the stepchildren as his own. I talked to him on the telephone when possible and then began to audio record my daily experiences and send the tapes to him. This exchange became my way of bonding with him as if he were sitting right there in my law office.

For Dad's seventy-fifth birthday, the family organized a surprise party at the country club in Auburn. While playing golf with him, I had to stall a bit so that all of his friends, and there were many, could gather around the eighteenth green. Like me, Dad was never much of stylish dresser except when he was in realtor mode. On that great day surrounded by loved ones he wore his multi-colored checkered slacks with a shirt that barely matched any of the colors of his pants.

I kept in touch for several weeks until, on a dark, rainy morning, my sister Anne called me with the news of Dad's passing. For about a year leading up to his fatal stroke, his health had been deteriorating. He was seventy-six at the time, and had lived a loving, caring life attending to nine children who knew their father/stepfather was always there for them. Like most children when a parent dies, I wished I had spent more time with my father. I loved him immeasurably and wondered if I had told him that enough times.

Over the next few days, memories of the times Dad and I had spent together flooded my mind. I remembered how he and my mom had rewarded my graduation from Purdue with a red Buick. A photograph shows the three of us standing by the car with huge smiles on our faces.

I remembered how terrible our Little League team was, and how it didn't matter. Dad and Mom were there for every game cheering us on. Dad bought me a Ted Willams three-finger mitt to use. It has traveled with me wherever I have gone. When I look at that mitt, I think of my dad. He was the best, and he and Mom are included in every prayer I've ever said.

When both your mother and father have passed, you begin to reflect on your life often. Finding independence and running around the country and the world had created many memorable moments, but I resented the trade-off of being away from family and friends. Mom had died so suddenly and at such a young age, and I missed her terribly. Then Dad was gone, and I had no one to guide my path or to talk to about things that really mattered. Since I wasn't much of a spiritual person then, there was no guidance from that end either. Some days I really wondered where I was headed, whether LA was the right place for me. Midwestern values like honesty and integrity were for the most part absent in Hollywood. I made some friends, but none like the solid ones I had grown up with in Auburn, during my days at Purdue and IU Law School, or while I was a defense lawyer in Indianapolis. If there was any woman who had been a mother figure, it was Alice Dye. She treated me like a son, complete with a good talking-to once in a while. If you didn't want a straight answer, you didn't ask Alice, which I later recognized as "tough love."

Some nights, I felt there was hole in my heart, that I was playing the entertainment game without much reason to do so other than the lure of fame. I certainly couldn't shake the temptation to stay the course while renting a guesthouse on Mulholland Drive high above Beverly Hills, owned by Hugh O'Brien, the actor who had played Wyatt Earp on television. He was past sixty at the time, but nevertheless entertained a number of young Hollywood star wannabes who hoped he might help them hit the big time. Hugh loved to skinny dip in his pool, and one evening a young beauty wandered over to the guesthouse while Hugh frolicked in the pool with another young beauty. The star-wannabe asked me whether she could trust him to make the connections he was promising. I couldn't lie and told her he couldn't, that his heart might be in the right place but that his time in the spotlight had passed. The girl thanked me for being honest, but I could tell she was very disappointed.

While living in that guesthouse, I was humiliated when I sat by the telephone for four straight days waiting for the general manager of the ABC affiliate to call me regarding a position as an on-air personality. He never called, and finally I realized I had been an idiot to believe he would call. Upset, I decided a nice run on Mulholland Drive would make me feel better. Instead, I was scared out of my wits when a brown German shepherd leaped out of the high grass along the road. Before I could scamper away, he bit me right in the ass. The wound wasn't deep, but the embarrassment was when I had to explain my injury to the nurse at the emergency room. Her first words were "drop your pants," and I could hear the giggles in the room full of doctors and nurses as I did.

Later that year, one that included the space shuttle Atlantis' maiden flight, San Francisco beckoned again when I was chosen to be one of six co-hosts—yes, six—on a nationally syndicated television program called *World of People*. Traveling around the Bay Area and some neighboring states, we covered ugly-dog contests, and reported on a reunion of the Beach Boys in Reno including pudgy, bloodshot-eyed drummer Dennis Wilson, who was incoherent from drugs during the interview, and who died shortly thereafter. He had it all: fame, money, more women than he could ever enjoy. But drugs had drained his brain and would not let go. Those who believe fame is a true celebration never understand that some people simply cannot handle it. It is a true blessing and curse at the same time.

For one program, I visited the Winchester Mystery House in San Jose where kids loved to open doors that led to nowhere. Then I was asked to be a judge at the Miss Nude California competition where we filmed the proceedings with utmost care. One can only imagine how difficult it was to keep eye contact during the interview process. As the day proceeded, I met a beautiful redhead and later had an "up close and personal" look at her freckles. This was the side of show business I liked the most.

The best part of being a *World of People* host was the ability to ride my bike to the studio from my wood-frame houseboat in Sausalito. When the tide was in, the boat rocked with a steady beat. I seldom saw neighbors; most were hermits who wanted nothing to do with the outside world. I liked that seclusion, and telling people I was living in a houseboat sounded cool. It fit with the image I wanted to project, that I was cool like a Hollywood type was supposed to be. Deep down, though, I was still Indiana Mark with good Midwestern values to guide me. But I didn't want to let people know that. In some ways, I was hiding behind a mask, but in California, with all its insecure people, that was the standard way to be. Later, my understanding about masks and insecurity would be embellished during the tough times.

During one crazed escapade on the houseboat, a *World of People* producer wanted to have some fun with a circumcision ceremony.

He dressed me appropriately, laid me on a table, and then photographed a huge, sharp knife cutting the head off a large, dead fish. You had to be there to appreciate the art. In no way was the segment meant to demean the true meaning of a sacred bris. It was just a bunch of us playing around, no ill intentions.

Joining us in the fun just a mile or so from downtown Sausalito was a lovely woman from nearby Novato. She had a young son and I was able to spend time with him. The potential for marriage was there, but the timing wasn't quite right for either the woman or me. But I knew I would not have hesitated becoming a stepfather if things had been a bit different. Some evenings, I sat on the houseboat dock and looked at the beauty of the sunsets over the nearby mountains. Was life passing me by, I wondered? Would there ever be a chance to have a family? Did it make sense to put off having a family? Would I regret it one day when I was alone?

More than that, I questioned whether I could commit to the emotional attachment necessary to share my life with someone. Several times, I had discussions with women about my inability to give up the independence I enjoyed. For whatever reason, among them immaturity, I simply was not able to commit, not able to give up the chance of meeting someone new and exciting, of experiencing what it would be like to be with her. On nights after a self-induced breakup, I would shake my head in disbelief. These were the lonely times, the ones bachelors never want to talk about.

Even though my private life was in turmoil, my entertainment career was blossoming. Within weeks after *World of People* ended, a producer named Mary Ann from the Disney Channel saw one of my stories and hired me to be "Mr. Science," a takeoff on the *Mr. Wizard* series. We filmed fifty episodes of *The Scheme of Things* even though

I had made Ds in science from high school through college. Our crew traveled all over appearing academic and important, while telling the kiddies who watched the channel how technical things worked, or why they didn't work. One time I dressed up in silly native costumes from various countries while at Epcot Center in Orlando (the worst one: a German yodeler complete with white knee socks). On camera, I also explained how the banana was a true wonder since it provided its own packaging. Heavy stuff.

While in San Francisco, a producer from *Entertainment Tonight* asked me to interview pop singer Cyndi Lauper (*Girls Just Want to Have Fun*) when she christened the opening of the new Hard Rock Café. I agreed, unaware that the interview would take place with her standing in a dumpster outside the restaurant. After making no sense whatsoever when she talked to me, the red-, green-, and purple-haired Cyndi peed at the other end of the dumpster behind some broken wooden slats as I watched from behind two piles of rubbish.

A friend who was a double for Marilyn Monroe introduced me to famed attorney Melvin Belli, defender of Errol Flynn, Mae West, Jack Ruby, the Rolling Stones, Mohammed Ali, and Jim and Tammie Faye Bakker. After getting to know him a bit, I pitched an idea called *The Belli Files*, which were essentially short television commentaries about the law. We filmed thirty episodes at his museum-like Montgomery Street offices. In July Belli asked me to go to the Major League Baseball All-Star game at Candlestick Park. With the top down, we rode in his gold Rolls-Royce across the Golden Gate Bridge as his silver locks blew in the wind. At the game, I watched people mob him in the stands like a rock star. He had gained notoriety after suing the Giants when the stadium seat warmers didn't work properly. Belli had legally "attached" (a legal term, which means to take possession of) the body of superstar Willie Mays until the Giants paid him ten thousand dollars in damages.

During the time we filmed the *Belli Files*, he and I became good friends. So much so that when I decided to create a program called *Trials and Tribulations*, a half-hour syndicated television show, he agreed to be a guest. From friends and supporters, we raised enough money to film what was called a pilot, a sample program. The show featured several segments, including an interview with a legal celebrity (Belli); a focus on a current trial of the week; consumer legal tips; and a segment called The Legal Mailbag where I answered letters from viewers that featured our mascot, The Legal Beagle, a dog who was supposed to carry letters from about ten feet away for me to open and answer. Unfortunately, during the taping of the pilot, the brown and white beagle we hired kept chasing after a crew member's cat, but he was cute and finally sat beside me as I opened the mail. The program concept, a true forerunner to what later would be called *Court TV*, was well-received. Dick Clark, the *American Bandstand* creator, and his production company, agreed to help secure television interest, and we came extremely close to landing a deal. But the idea was just a bit ahead of its time, and finally we gave up any chance of its finding a television network or syndication home.

Having attempted to become a television star without much luck, an entertainment attorney with little success, and a producer with no shows (the *Belli Files* and *Trials and Tribulations* were both flops), I decided to see if celebrity management might be my calling. In 1986, at age forty-one, I moved back to LA from San Francisco and hooked up with a manager/attorney/producer named Larry Thompson. He asked me to join his firm, one that managed the careers of such stars as William Devane (star of *Knots Landing*),

Charlene Tilton (*Dallas*), William Shatner (*Star Trek*), Jamie Farr (*M.A.S.H.*), and Donna Mills (*Knots Landing*). During a dinner with Devane, he used more cusswords in an hour than I had heard in a lifetime. He was a hard case, a diehard polo player, but the language hit home with brute force.

My experience with Donna Mills, an angelic actress who was sweet and loveable, was quite the opposite, so much so that I had a crush on her. She talked very slowly and deliberately, each word carefully chosen and executed. When she visited our office, I just stood and stared at her like a groupie, unable to believe someone could be that beautiful.

For a time, I kidded myself that Donna might be interested in me. One of the fellows in the office told her about my crush, and to my amazement, she agreed to have lunch. I was so nervous I dropped my fork into a glass of water, which splashed over the warm bread basket. She laughed, but I knew she probably thought I was a dunderhead. Being so shaky reminded me of a lawyer friend named Kent who was a bit naïve about women and was even less sophisticated socially. When the waiter approached the table where he and his date were sitting in a cozy French restaurant, and asked what wine he preferred, my friend panicked and blurted out "Chateaubriand," apparently the only French word he knew. To his credit, the waiter never flinched at the mention of a thick cut of tenderloin, and simply brought my friend a bottle of red wine. Whether the date knew of my friend's faux pas, I wasn't told, but that story made rounds for years to come.

My hopes of any romance with Donna were never realized. She and I talked for a while, but I was small potatoes, and soon "the trades," the name used for such publications as *Variety* and *The Hollywood Reporter*, reported that she had found her true love.

Later, a friend arranged a date with Sally Struthers, the frizzy-haired co-star of *All in the Family*. Like Donna, she loved to laugh, which brought me much joy.

Within a few minutes after I agreed to join his management firm, Larry Thompson told me to rent a tuxedo. This first in my life was necessary because I was about to attend the Golden Globe Awards. One minute I had been sitting in Larry's office, and the next I was sitting at a table with Larry near several A-list stars including Diane Keaton, Jack Nicholson, Steve McQueen and the like. I wasn't sure what was causing my heart to nearly burst, the tight shirt collar around my neck, or a brain that could not believe what I was seeing. Who was guiding my life anyway? Who was providing me with moments of such a special nature that they seemed like a dream? Who or what, I kept asking myself, unable to understand how I could be in the presence of some of the biggest stars in Hollywood. Later, I sat near a restaurant table where Diane Keaton was chatting with a movie producer. Her face shone like it had a million stars all around it as she ate her Cobb salad. I wanted to scoot over and say hello. When she noticed me staring, I thought she might bark at me, but she simply smiled. I suppose being starstruck is not a crime.

I was especially reminded of how cutthroat show business is when I accompanied Charlene Tilton, who played Lucy Ewing on the hit series *Dallas*, to an audition. A short woman with a soft face and a kindly way about her, she asked me to pray with her just before her audition for a small-time stage play a year or so after *Dallas'* cancellation.

One who would survive and have a long-lasting career, however, was Canadian-born actor William Shatner. I met him after he had retired from his Captain Kirk role. I felt that he was not only a good actor, but one who understood the business part of show business. With Larry Thompson's guidance, and Shatner's moxie, the two planned for the long term, one resulting in shows such as *T.J. Hooker* and then *Boston Legal*. His good-humored personality also won him the spokesman role for Priceline, the Internet travel site.

Working for Larry had its benefits, but working for anyone was never my forte. I was too much the "risk/reward" type of fellow, one whose independent nature made me want to strike out on my own. Feast or famine, that was my credo, and during these years, while the work was stimulating, my bank account never blossomed.

I thought producing might be the trick, whether television or movies. What is a producer? At the time no one really could define it accurately, but it is basically the person who packages the whole product: the writers, the script, the actors, the director and so forth. Those who also help raise the money for production are called executive producers. At one point, I met with Robert Culp, the lively co-star with Bill Cosby of the popular program *I Spy*. He was searching for producer opportunities like me but even his name couldn't open doors because he was typecast as an actor.

Ever resourceful, I optioned a couple of scripts and even though I heard the proverbial Hollywood "We just love it" words of hope, nothing worked. No matter, I continued to try, ever the optimistic one. Producers all over town were kind enough to meet with me, including those on the Disney and Paramount lots. I met Don Penny, a real character who loved to wear combat boots while smoking a big cigar, and he invited me to work with him on the Twentieth Century lot. I not only accepted, but spent several nights sleeping on the office couch when I was between living quarters. Sometimes the security, suspicious of anyone hanging around after midnight, would flash a light into the office, startling me. By six in the morning, I was awake and soon headed for the Fox commissary. Movie and television stars abounded. I also loved to watch film crews using production sets specifically built for different movie locations. To say I was caught up in show business is an understatement. I was truly smitten and determined to become a big shot like those who flocked to the commissary each day.

I used one film project, *Diving In*, a story about a high school diver afraid of heights who wants to overcome his fear, which gained some interest at the independent film company New World Pictures, as an excuse to visit France for the Cannes Film Festival. Located on the French Rivera bordering the beautiful waters of the Mediterranean where multi-million-dollar yachts dot the surface, the tiny town sparkles with life during a festival that lures many of the most famous names in film. Premieres of new films that will debut later on around the world are showcased between parties that last until dawn. Since a producer named Jerry was a friend, I attended a premiere for *Going to the Chapel*, a film he was pushing. Sitting next to directors, producers and a few stars from his film was mesmerizing. I kept wondering what the hell I was doing there, but nevertheless drank the champagne and ate hors d'œuvres sporting names I could not even pronounce.

Months later, Jerry invited me to a party in Brentwood, just across the 405 freeway from Westwood, Hollywood, and Los Angeles. When I walked in, standing there was O. J. Simpson, nattily attired in what must have been a five-thousand-dollar suit, and his wife Nicole Brown Simpson. As I glanced across the room, she was so beautiful, so radiant it was almost like a stage spotlight hovered overhead and she was the only woman at the party. I noticed others, including a celebrity or two, staring at Nicole as she moved with grace toward a famous producer who hugged her tightly. Her beauty was simply beyond comparison. She lit up the room as if walking on air.

To be considered "in" in the entertainment business, it was necessary to make the rounds of the fancy restaurants and bars where one may be seen in the company of celebrities. I thus visited such famous watering holes as the Beverly Hills Hotel Polo Lounge, The Grill in Beverly Hills, Morton's, and Le Dome on Sunset Strip. Since it was hip to "take meetings" even if there was nothing to meet about, I played the game as the normal course of business. During these meetings, anyone trying to be anybody with stature had to talk about the "next project," a film, a television show, anything down the line because you had to have a next project even if there was no project.

What everyone wanted to hear said were the magic words, "Your project has been greenlighted," meaning a studio or television network had given the go-ahead for production, as opposed to landing in what is called "development hell," which I experienced firsthand after co-writing a screenplay with Ted Key, the creator of the famous newspaper cartoon series *Hazel*, about a hard-boiled maid with a kind heart. Creative Artists Agency, one of the big three at the time along with William Morris and ICM, had handed me the opportunity, which permitted my entry into the prestigious Writer's Guild of America. But the script we wrote, one that our agent thought was pretty damn good to the point of interesting former actor and then director Penny Marshall, was rewritten, and then rewritten again, opening the door to development hell. The script really wasn't bad, but in Hollywood, two novices like Ted and me didn't have much power. We would need bigger screenwriter "names" to give the project a boost. When Ted and I read the new script, it had lost what we called "the Hazel attitude"—a feisty sort who meant what she said. Finally, the project was killed, dead like so many others.

Living in la-la land sounded good when I told friends about it, but inside I knew this life was not for me. I was yearning to settle down, to gain some roots, and I even thought I had found the right woman with whom to share my life. But she was caught up in the Hollywoodland scene as well, and while I really cared for her, we squabbled about our differences regarding future plans. I was confused about what to do, and like many others, when times are tough, I decided to seek some sort of spiritual guidance. To that end, in yet another inexplicable defining moment, I joined the Beverly Hills Presbyterian Church (BHPC) on Rodeo Drive in an attempt to gain some sort of spiritual foundation. The rollercoaster personal relationship was the initial reason for attending, but maybe I figured that with God on my side I might actually survive, if I chose to, in the tough entertainment world where it was difficult to gain any success, tougher to stay successful, and usually a mental and financial disaster when the success faded away. I cried myself to sleep many nights as I tried to make sense of what was occurring in my life.

At the church, the minister Jim Morrison's sermons calmed my worried soul. For the first time in my life, I actually became quite involved in church activities. When someone was needed to organize and direct a play about Bible parables, I volunteered. Watching the kids perform to a standing-room-only audience was a pure delight. Once again, I thought about the potential to marry and have children, but during that time, as I approached my mid-forties, I couldn't even take care of myself, let alone a wife and kids, especially when it came to finances. When Father's Day arrived and the church held a special ceremony in celebration, I not only felt sad and alone, but missed my dad more than ever. If only he and Mom had been alive, they could have helped me decide what to do with my life. I was a confused mess and I needed their guidance more than ever.

One holiday season, when a member of the church, famed actor James Stewart (*It's a Wonderful Life, Mr. Smith Goes to Washington, Vertigo*), read aloud the story of Christmas, I felt as if God were standing right before us. An idea to research the stories behind the music of Christmas struck me. When I discovered intriguing facts about such classics as *Silent Night, Little Town of Bethlehem, and The First Noel,* I decided to pitch the show to minister Jim and choir director Nick. Both thought the idea had some merit, whereupon I asked if we could present it to Mr. Stewart (I never referred to him as James or Jimmy or Stewart) to see whether he might have interest in participating, possibly as the program host. One can only imagine how nervous I was when I met Mr. Stewart, a stately, impressive figure, one who was the center of attention anytime he entered a room with an unforgettable voice—distinctive, decisive, and mesmerizing all at once.

As I sat across from Mr. Stewart, my hands were shaking so hard I could hardly keep still. My throat was dry and the first words out of my mouth were unsteady. But after hearing me stutter my intentions, he simply looked at me, paused as my heart nearly stopped, and said, "You bet. Good idea." With that, he rose, shook my hand, one I did not wash for the rest of the day, and left. I sat in a daze, unable to comprehend what had just happened. The great James Stewart was going to host a program based on my ideas. That evening, a bottle of wine, a good one at that, helped me enjoy yet another mystical experience. The next morning I called Nick, the choir director, to make sure the meeting had not been a dream. He laughed before asking me, "Okay, what do we do now?"

Armed with Mr. Stewart's blessing, I took the idea to a respected producer named Woody Fraser. He had hired me at *Good Morning America* and was well known for the hit television series *That's Incredible*. Using Mr. Stewart's name as a calling card, we rounded up some of his friends including George Burns, Burt Reynolds, Lucille Ball, Walter Matthau, Bobby McFerrin, Lee Greenwood, and Denise Williams. When we filmed the opening of the show on a studio lot with Burns, who had achieved fame with his late wife Gracie Allen, the ninety-year-old captivated us with jokes and laughter of a man fifty years younger while calling me "kid." Equipped with his ever present cigar, Burns, in his monologue, teased Mr. Stewart about opening the show. It was easy to see how much mutual respect existed between these two legendary performers. Burns' lines, as he lounged in a cushy chair, cigar in hand, read: "Jimmy Stewart asked me to open the show. I asked him why. He said, 'you have spent more Christmases in Beverly Hills than anybody, including Santa Claus.'"

On a warm afternoon and into a chilly evening, we taped the remaining segments of what would be called *A Beverly Hills Christmas with James Stewart* for Fox Broadcasting. Two fond memories stand out. While filming, a stage hand told me Mr. Stewart asked to see me outside the church. I walked to where he was standing afraid something was wrong. He shook my hand, commenting, "Everything looks good," and then added, "What can I do to help?" I blurted, "Nothing sir, nothing at all. Thank you for everything." He said, "Fine, okay, just let me know if there is anything I can do to help." As he walked away, I just shook my head. Here was one of the most revered men in the world, not only for his superb acting skills, but also because of his kindness. As the taping wound down, Mr. Stewart sat next to me in one of the church pews. We watched Burt Reynolds, his toupee securely in place, banter with his wife, the beautiful Loni Anderson of *WKRP in Cincinnati* television fame. Walter Matthau, Oscar Madison in the *Odd Couple*, sat nearby and laughed at their antics.

After the taping, Mr. Stewart and I became good friends and exchanged letters. I even visited him in his Wilshire Avenue office. He treated me like a son and I relished his interest in me. Few people in life ever impressed me as much as Mr. Stewart did. At one point, he asked me to call him Jimmy, but it just didn't feel right to do so.

My second fond memory from the Christmas show involves Lucille Ball, better known as "Lucy." Right before taping, she called in a frantic state. Worried about what advanced age had done to her looks, she made me promise there would be no close-ups when she read *The Story of Christmas* with Mr. Stewart. She shouldn't have worried; she looked very beautiful and her voice blended perfectly with Mr. Stewart's. When the audience gathered for the taping (only one "take" was necessary) and heard the two legends read together, I was certain they agreed that it was like God and Mrs. God speaking. It sure sounded like it to me. Later on, I discovered their special performance became a YouTube fixture. Soon after the taping, I framed a photograph of me standing in between Mr. Stewart and Burt Reynolds. I'm the one wearing the madras shirt, the one with the big smile, the one who can't believe his good fortune.

Uplifted over the success of the Christmas program, but discouraged with continually knocking on doors trying to make a living, I took a long walk along Santa Monica Beach. I decided then to move back to Indiana near my family and true friends. I felt it would be a step backwards professionally, but I was homesick for what I called "real people," those who could be counted on through good and bad times, those who were straight shooters like my friends the Dyes, Scott Montross, Billy Keller, and Judy Deputy. California is a magical place, but most people only say they are your friends, but aren't, and who can blame them when the stakes are so high and everyone wants to be rich, famous and powerful.

Throughout my up-and-down television career, people who knew me wondered how I had been so blessed. On the surface, I appeared to have it made, but there was a void inside me that could not be filled. I truly missed genuine, caring people, most of whom gathered in the heartland of America, or the mountains to the immediate west. The experiences I had would never leave me, but I needed some fresh air far from the Hollywood craziness. Those who learned of my decision to leave California for Indiana thought I was as mixed up as when I had left Indiana for Colorado and beyond years earlier. But whatever Spirit was guiding me along had something very special in mind to enhance my life, something that would help prepare me for a miracle down the road.

CHAPTER FOUR

The Stepfather

"You can't put your bag up there," I heard a woman say as I stood in the aisle preceding a scheduled flight from Austin, Texas to Indianapolis in 1989.

Ready to argue the point, I looked back and saw Chris, a woman I had known during my days as a defense lawyer more than ten years earlier, smiling at me. When we first met, I was too smitten with my job, and didn't pay enough attention to the fact that I had discovered a wonderful woman who loved me dearly. The romance wilted, which had been my fault. She and I had lost touch, but I never lost the good feelings I had for her, even after I quit practicing criminal defense law and darted off to Aspen.

I was coming back from Texas, where I had been visiting an intriguing fellow named Sam Grogg, when Chris spotted me on the plane. Sam had started a film fund that invested money in many films, among them *Kiss of the Spider Woman* and *Trip to Bountiful*, in order to diversify risk. Both films had been successful, financially and critically. My interest in filmmaking made me feel there was an opportunity to duplicate what Sam had established in Texas in Indiana.

After returning to my home state, a savvy banker and I started a similar fund. We raised a considerable amount of money, and discovered a young director looking for work; the director owned the rights to a good script about some high school kids who uncover a scandal in a governor's office. Suddenly, I had added another occupation to my fast-growing list: executive producer.

The film, called *Freeze Frame*, starring Shannen Doherty of *Beverly Hills 90210* fame, also featured a few mid-level stars. The most memorable part of the experience was trying to patch up a spat when Shannen, who was quite young at the time, fell madly in love with one of the producers. They had a behind-the-scenes love affair until he dumped her, or she dumped him. For days, both of them sulked and I finally had to patch things up so we could actually complete production. Regardless, the film was well received by the critics and had a good video run. A highlight for me was an appearance as a high school English teacher. Alfred Hitchcock, the famous director who always inserted himself into his films, would have been proud of me. I wore a snazzy brown corduroy jacket, a tie, and really looked the part for my screen debut.

The decent success of *Freeze Frame* led to the production of a second film, *Diving In*, when a swell guy, Mickey Maurer, an Indianapolis financier, decided to finance the film I couldn't get produced in Hollywood. The mid-level stars included Bert Young of *Rocky*; Kristy Swanson; Matt Lattanzi, the husband of singer Olivia Newton John; and my friend Richard Johnson, the brilliant stage actor/producer from England. In my second appearance on the big screen, yours truly played a janitor at the high school swimming pool where the kids trained. When the Burt Young character walked into the area, I was supposed to mumble something about the pool temperature, but during several takes, I couldn't remember the eight words I was supposed to say. Burt laughed, but it was a sinister laugh. I kept thinking of him in the *Rocky* films, how he was a tough guy who could beat me up if I continued to flub my lines.

The end result was mediocre at best, but the film did a little business in the theaters before heading straight for Paramount Home Video. In any case, the premiere was worth it considering all the glitz and glamour, Hollywood style, and limousines that Indianapolis could muster. Best of all was sharing the fun and excitement with not only my immediate family, but with five new people in my life: Chris and her four children; Kimberly, who was ten years old at the time, and eight-year-old triplet boys Kent, Kyle, and Kevin.

When I had first met her kids at a Chuck E Cheese's, they grabbed my pants leg and wouldn't let go. Immediately I realized they were thirsting for attention. For days, I walked on air, looking forward to seeing them at every turn.

Months later, after Chris and I rekindled the fondness we had for one another years earlier, the four kids became my stepchildren and I, their stepfather. Suddenly the reason for a Spirit's guiding me back to Indiana made itself quite clear and I didn't hesitate in my new role as the stepfather to four children, a daunting task to many. Now I had the chance to be part of a family and to love the children as my own, just as my father had done with his new family after my mother's passing. Now, I thought, I could put into practice all that I have learned over the years from watching parents and their kids, from being a big brother, and from working with the group of church youngsters at the Beverly Hills church.

From the moment I met the kids on through a marriage sancti-
fied by Joy, a justice of the peace in Florida during a trip to Disney
World, I had a constant smile on my face, even despite my knowing,
knowing for certain, that I was never to be a biological father to a
child, never to be called "Dad" or "Daddy," never to utter the words
"son," "daughter," "grandson" or "granddaughter." By marrying a
woman who could no longer bear children, I had given up that right
through a choice I consciously made. I truly believed then, as any
newly married man does, that the marriage would last forever.

Because they loved their father, Chris' divorce was a rough experience for the kids and she and I tried to make the tough times
better by being there for them at every turn. We were a family, one
that stuck together as we sought new experiences while the days and
months passed. Kimberly (when I first met her she had a cute
black and white rabbit named Newspaper), had vivid memories of
growing up that included adventures during our California and
Colorado trips such as bungee-jumping and riding in a multi-colored
hot air balloon. Despite her small-sized stature, she was also a catcher
on the girl's high school softball team. One time she wrecked my
Chevy Blazer, but by the grace of God, she was not hurt.

Later, Kimberly, like most rebellious teenagers, defiantly told me,
"I am going to a Grateful Dead concert in Michigan" instead of asking
for permission, only to be shocked when instead of me saying "no"
to the idea of such a thing, I merely said, "Would you like to use the
van?" She stammered, "I guess," and walked away shaking her head.

Kimberly, the independent one, lost her way for a while but then,
with the help of her birth father Jerry, ended up at Xavier College
where she worked hard and graduated. Patience was the byword with
Kimberly. Chris and I understood that she just needed time to feel

good about herself, to know that she could succeed after having been somewhat overshadowed by the attention her triplet brothers received.

Being a stepfather was tricky business and I never attempted to be the children's father, but instead more of an uncle, or an older brother. Kimberly helped me try to learn to swim and soon I was taking the triplets fishing for the first time. We bowled and played pool. I wrestled with all three on the floor, and took them on the train to New York City for the Macy's Thanksgiving Day parade. During the trip, the triplets "operated" on me as I lay on one of the seats. I believe it was a fake heart transplant but it could have been a liver extraction. We laughed all morning as we had when Kimberly, the triplets, and I had slowly crawled up the narrow, winding steps at the Statue of Liberty as a stiff wind swayed the iconic monument from side to side.

Displaying my little kid side, I showed them how much fun it was to eat birthday cake with their hands. I wrote poems to them, hid Easter eggs, helped the triplets build a tree house, taught them how to whistle, and how to hold a fork correctly. Soon I was known as the "fork patrol," a reference to my correcting the triplets' friends when they violated the "fork rule."

During the winter months, we attended Indiana Pacer playoff games and rode around in the car honking the horn when they won. Then the whole family attended an Indianapolis Colts game where the triplets met placekicker Dean Biacussi, both after the game and at our home when he visited us. I had invited him over after he told me that he was interested in an acting career after his football career was over. When the triplets became enamored with kicking field goals, we erected a goal post in the front yard where they, especially Kevin, kicked, and kicked, and kicked some more during afternoons when I played quarterback and the three boys played wide receiver. I treasured hitting fly balls to them on the front lawn and playing catch like my father used to do with me. Chris and I were there for every school meeting and never missed an athletic event in which the children participated. Most days, I either took the kids to school, or picked them up. They could rely on me; I considered myself a rock in their lives, one who would never leave them. Some friends marveled at how well I had adapted to stepfatherhood, but I had been preparing for parenting my whole life.

By the end of each school year, we took an annual family trip to Chicago where everyone sat with me in the rain and cold at Wrigley Field and cheered my beloved, suffering Cubs. We visited the Shedd Aquarium and the Field Museum and enjoyed the lights and magic of Michigan Avenue shops. Watching the kids learn and grow warmed my heart.

Although I wasn't a churchgoer, as I had been in Beverly Hills, I had a wonderful appreciation for how the Spirit was blessing me. Each Christmas Eve, we all piled into a car and attended a service at the local Christian church. I'm sure the minister wondered where we were the rest of the year. When I slept at night, I had a peaceful feeling. The higher Spirit guiding me had guided me right to this family, a broken family where I felt needed and loved. When I wrote in my journal at night, I thanked the Good Lord for His blessings. Even if I was not a churchgoer, I knew God was in my life.

Kimberly was closer to her mother and father than to me. As expected, most of my memories from those days revolve around the triplets. During the summers, I helped them collect baseball cards, and took them to the World Series one year when Cincinnati played Oakland. I organized an amateur team so they could play basketball.

I coached them when we formed a team for the summer Gus Macker league, and one year the triplets and a friend nearly won their division. We all loved meeting giant-sized Kent Benson, the starting center on one of Indiana University's NCAA basketball championship teams, when he attended one of the Macker sessions. The triplets were very short at the time and it was very amusing to see them dribble under Kent's legs as he laughed at the fun they were having.

One spring, when Kimberly was deciding what colleges she wanted to attend, I helped coach the triplets' Little League baseball team. I also took them to pro motorbike races where they fell in love with the sport and met champion racer Jeremy McGrath. Soon after this, we purchased a small orange motorbike for them to try and they raced it round and round the property as our dogs, six at one point (Snickers, Bach, Shadow, Reggie Miller, Peanut Butter, and White Sox), barked at them like they were crazy. Realizing the triplets *were* crazy about riding, we bought three new small Hondas, and they raced and raced some more, finally at competitions where they scared the bejesus out of their mother and me. But they loved the thrill and so we kept traveling to competitions around the area. We built a short racetrack in our front yard and all was well until Kyle attempted too big of a jump and landed on his back. I scurried home from a California trip to his bedside while the Good Lord protected him from serious injury. At that point their mother said enough was enough. But the triplets started riding again and I loved to watch them speed up and down on a larger track that they had built with their buddies and me in the woods.

All the while I kept in mind the lessons learned from my mother and father. When Father's Day rolled around, I appreciated Kimberly and the triplets' kind words and gestures before they left to see their real father. It hurt, of course, since while I had the responsibility of watching over them every day and night, their father was able to enjoy them without the problems one faces with raising kids. But there I was truly blessed too, especially since Kimberly and "the boys," as Chris and I called them at times, were, for the most part, a joy to parent. Someone once asked me what it was like to raise triplets. I responded that the triplets got along so well I never witnessed them fighting. If they would have been unruly, I added, I would have been in a mental institution. To show how much they loved each other, when Kyle made the seventh grade basketball team, and Kevin and Kent were disappointed that they had not, Kevin and Kent still joined me in supporting Kyle throughout the season. When one boy had a great day racing motorbikes, and the others had a tough ride, no one griped but instead congratulated their brother on the win.

Dealing with four kids on a daily basis taught me patience and understanding. I watched what I said, and how I acted, since I knew they were sponges who soaked up all that was happening around them. When there was a decision to be made, I simply said, "Use good judgment," words I learned from my parents. The kids sometimes tired of that, but I trusted them and wanted them to think for themselves.

When television programs such as *Dawson's Creek* were popular, I sat with Kimberly and the triplets and watched along with them. I helped with homework and I took books to school when they forgot them. I even accepted an offer to join the county sheriff's merit board. In the event that any problems arose involving law enforcement, my contacts there would prove helpful in protecting them, which is how I learned of Kimberly's auto accident minutes after it happened.

The home we owned was located on sixty acres in southern Indiana just a half hour from Bloomington. It was a log house with a pond nestled behind it. Ducks and geese wandered around and the dogs tried to chase them when they could. Then, just weeks after we had purchased the home, without warning, it burned down when an electrical malfunction in one of the cars parked in the garage caused a fire. I was in Indianapolis at the time, and drove my car at breakneck speed toward Nashville, about an hour south of the capital city, when I heard the news. How relieved I was when I saw Chris and the four kids bunched up in a fireman's car. Her quick thinking when she smelled smoke had saved all of their lives. I also believed my guardian angels had protected everyone.

Our family lived in a rental for a few weeks afterwards. There a mother cat decided to have her babies under my arm while I slept. When I awoke, the kids watched with amazement as six or seven kittens appeared in a little under an hour. Then the cat went on her way; she was done with me.

While our main house was being rebuilt with insurance funds, we moved into a guesthouse a hundred yards or so to the south of where the main house had stood. The guesthouse, one I later turned into a writing studio, had been a large motorcycle shed for the previous owner. It had a basketball court behind it where the triplets and I played and played and played some more. In the evenings, their friends visited and I felt honored when asked to join them. I could hold my own because the "old man," as they called me, could hit three pointers with regularity. The one rule I imposed was: whenever the kids asked me to do something with them, I cancelled anything else and did it. Ninety-nine percent of the time I was there with them when they woke up, and I was there when they went to bed.

During his senior year, Kevin broke his arm during practice. Day by day, I rebounded for him after it healed. He fought hard to recover and I was as proud as any stepfather when he rejoined the basketball team and scored a point in a tournament game. I recalled the days when my father encouraged me to play sports, especially Little League baseball. Now I was encouraging my stepsons to play. Just playing catch with them was the best joy; any father or stepfather will tell you that.

The triplets performed decently well in school even though they never wanted to read a book longer than one hundred pages. But the time spent with them and Kimberly was special as we traveled, along with our friend Becky Miller, to the Pacific Ocean near San Diego, to Disneyland where we met Mickey and Minnie, and to Aspen where I showed them my old haunts from the 1970s and they rode the ski lifts to the top of Aspen Mountain. We rode horses on a mountain trail and Kimberly flew up in a multi-colored, hot air balloon in Snowmass as we looked up at her in awe. Kent made us all laugh when he meant to say "maneuver," and instead said "manure."

During the winters, we traveled to Florida with my wife's family to a beachfront area on the west coast. We also visited Disney World where my screaming "Oh, s***!" during a wild rollercoaster ride made the kids laugh. Even a whirl on the Mad Tea Cups or Pirates of the Caribbean made me dizzy. Later, I took the triplets and their friend Jon to the 1996 Summer Olympics in Atlanta where they followed the track and field events, and basketball. The Spirit protecting me and the boys was in action once again when we left one hour prior to the tragic bombing in the Olympic Park where we could have been killed.

Without a regret, I enjoyed those years when I felt as if the children were my children even though they were not. Nevertheless, the kids treated me with respect and I loved them dearly. They kept me young and I relished my new life as a parent and a friend during the most exciting time of my life to date. Whenever someone saw the triplets or Kimberly and me together and said something like, "Wow, your kids are so polite," I quickly responded, "They are my stepchildren" to correct the mistake. I often told people that perhaps there should be a "Stepfather's Day," or a "Stepmother's Day," to honor those who step in and play the role of substitute father or mother.

Regardless of my parental title, the Spirit directing my life had prepared me to be a stepfather, and I was proud of the effort I put forth. I had not always been the most responsible person, but I had dedicated myself to raising the kids, and people who knew me gave me high marks. I do, however, regret how I treated the children's father Jerry at times. Instead of including him in the family as I should have, I purposely kept him at a distance. I had reasons for doing so, but I should have been more understanding, more compassionate, more willing to listen to his side of the story about family matters.

I was proud of how both Jerry and Chris' family treated me. They may have wondered whether a fellow in his late forties who had been a vagabond could handle parenthood, but they couldn't have been more supportive. I became close to Chris' father and stepmother after Chris' mother, a true saint of a woman, passed away. Chris' sister and her husband and her brother and his wife also became good friends. I cherished this extended family since I had little contact with my own brother and sisters. I became so involved with raising the kids that I forgot my birth family, a mistake I later regretted.

In 1992, the year Bill Clinton replaced George H.W. Bush as president, heavyweight boxing champion Mike Tyson was indicted for allegedly raping a young beauty queen in Indianapolis. Interested in the trial as a potential journalist, I wrote to Pat Gifford, the trial judge whom I knew from my days when she was a prosecutor and I was a defense counsel. Pat was aware of my Hollywood experience and asked me, in another defining moment, to handle the media for the case. I not only did so but also became a legal analyst for several networks including ABC, CNN, and ESPN. I began writing a column for *USA Today* and correctly predicted Tyson would be convicted despite the sketchy evidence. He never had a chance from the second his manager, Don King, hired Vincent Foster, a Washington, DC tax expert and the worst defense lawyer in the world.

When Tyson first heard the word "guilty" spoken by Judge Gifford, I watched from my courtroom seat as his head cocked to the side like he had been hit with a thunderous right cross. He whispered, "Oh, man," and slumped down in his seat. Tyson was now a convicted rapist.

I noticed that just before the verdict, Tyson sat alone, his bulk hanging over the sides of a chair at the counsel table. His lawyers had been drinking champagne and eating a tasty steak dinner at a fancy nearby restaurant awaiting the outcome of the trial. Throughout, I had watched Tyson closely. Once, when I began to walk through the door to the outer courtroom office, he approached. What made an impression was how small he was in stature, but how menacing he looked. I quickly stepped aside and let him pass. I wasn't about to be flicked to the floor by the so-called "baddest man on the planet."

During the trial, I included the triplets by having them visit the courthouse where they had their photograph taken with Tyson before his conviction. Just as my dad had done when I was young, the triplets were a part of everything I did.

Alarmed at the injustice I felt had tarnished the trial on many levels, I decided to write a book about the case called *Down for the Count*. It questioned whether a black celebrity could get a fair trial in the Midwest, which I highly doubted. When a publisher decided to publish the book, I added another profession to my resume: author, despite no real training other than writing legal briefs and columns for *USA Today* and stories for the *Aspen Daily News*.

Most book reviews across the country were terrific, but one Indianapolis reviewer lambasted it under the headline, "Shaw's book on Tyson worthless." Well-reviewed books received five stars, but this reviewer granted me none. After scaring my dogs by screaming in agony, I regrouped after discovering the reviewer had a grudge to bear since I had not given him credit for a quote of his I used in the book. Instead of crying foul, I decided, "I'll just write another damn book." And there was one just waiting for me after I traveled to the Dominican Republic where I had played golf with Pete and Alice Dye at Teeth of the Dog, a wondrous course with eight holes bordering the beautiful waters of the Caribbean. While there, Pete asked me to play in a tournament at La Romana Country Club, another of his magical courses. During the round, he told me I could not hit a certain shot to a par five since I was a "dumbass" by not understanding how he had designed the hole. He was right. Fascinated, I said, "We need to write this down; golfers need to know how you design your famous courses."

After interviewing Pete and Alice, a gifted course designer in her own right and the mastermind behind the infamous "island green" 17th hole at the TPC Sawgrass course in Florida where the PGA professionals play the Players Championship, Chris and I headed off to Scotland to emulate Pete and Alice's trip there in the 1960s. While there, I chopped my way around and through the gorse, a tough grass that snares the ball and never lets go, and deadly, deep pot bunkers on such mystical courses as Carnoustie, Dornach, Turnberry, Prestwick, and the most mystical of all, St. Andrews. Even a driving, sideways rainstorm could not dampen the enthusiasm I felt when I heard the starter say, "Play away." Later, when anyone asked me how good a player I was at the time, I just told them, "I parred the road hole," the famous 17th where so many British Open championships have been won and lost.

While researching the book, Pete introduced me to sandy-haired Jack Nicklaus at lunch (Nicklaus had a tuna sandwich; Pete and I had ham and Swiss). I sat between these two giants of golf as they chatted about their love for the game. Nicklaus off the course reminded me of Nicklaus on the course: very meticulous, and methodical when he talked about his approach to playing, and to designing golf courses. The latter had begun when he invited Pete to co-design Harbor Town Golf Links on Hilton Head Island. That jewel, despite its short length, remains one of the great golf courses in the world.

Nine months later, our book *Bury Me In A Pot Bunker* was born. Soon thereafter, a translated version was released in Japan. Many years later, I coaxed Alice Dye into helping her write a book called *From Birdies to Bunkers*. Alice, a top-notch amateur golfer in addition to her prowess as a golf course architect alongside Pete, provided tips about the game that helped beginners and veterans alike.

Bury Me In A Pot Bunker was a good success all around and had jump-started my writing career. After its publication Pete would call and I'd head for the local airport where one of his clients' private jets would whisk us off to places like Kiawah, South Carolina; Park City, Utah; or Kohler, Wisconsin. At each stop, I watched firsthand Pete's magical talents. What amazed me was how he actually created holes using his feet to feel the land on each prospective hole. Like the course designers of old in Scotland, he massaged the course into the earth so as to take advantage of the natural contours.

Always accompanying us was his dog Sixty. Pete gave the dog this name after paying twenty dollars for the dog, twenty dollars for the collar, and twenty dollars for the license. Sixty became so well known as Pete's co-passenger that many of the airports reported when Sixty was about to land. During a later trip to Kiawah Island where the Ryder Cup was played, one of my duties was to care for Sixty while Pete worked on the course. When Sixty wanted a drink, I filled a Dixie cup from the golf cart water jug. Pete saw this and said, "C'mon, Mark, just let him drink from the jug." I did, and then Pete chuckled all afternoon when several of the course officials including the golf professional, unbeknownst to them, drank from the same water jug as Sixty had.

With a terrific wife to love me, four kids to watch grow and blossom, six dogs to keep us company, and the opportunity to be an author, I was living my dream. Over the next few years, I wrote several more books, including one with famed aviator R.A. "Bob" Hoover for Simon and Schuster entitled *Forever Flying*. Lee Bailey introduced me to Bob, renowned as a World War II hero who began his flying career at age fifteen. During the war, he was shot down by the Germans and imprisoned. He then escaped, stole the same type of Messerschmitt that shot him down, and flew to freedom amongst a barrage of friendly fire. After spending several years as a top-notch test pilot alongside Chuck Yeager, Bob, known for wearing a wide-brimmed straw hat, became the world's foremost aerobatic pilot.

As the book showcased, aviation hero Jimmy Doolittle believed Bob was "the greatest stick-and-rudder man who ever lived," largely because he could dance a P-51 Mustang Fighter across the sky and then land it on a dime.

Bob was a true American hero and I was proud to be able to help with telling his story. It was a challenge prying any emotion out of Bob, especially when he described one of his planes catching on fire at twenty thousand feet as no big deal. When I repeatedly asked him, "How did you feel while the plane was spiraling out of control with flames all around?" he would just smile and in that Southern drawl of his, respond, "I guess it was a little hectic." Not exactly the response I had expected because if it had been me in that plane, I am sure I would have peed my pants, or worse.

When I spoke to Yeager, another aviation hero, requesting that he write the book's foreword, he did so immediately. Like Bob, Yeager was a no-nonsense, humble guy. He was very serious describing to me how Bob had been in the "chase plane" taking photographs when Yeager became the first man to fly faster than the speed of sound on October 14, 1947, the same flight that Tom Wolfe chronicled in his book *The Right Stuff.*

When I read baseball legend Mickey Mantle's book, *My Favorite Year, 1956*, the chapter entitled "Perfect" intrigued me. It described New York Yankee pitcher Don Larsen's perfect game during the 1956 World Series, the only one of its kind. I was fascinated by the story and flew to the San Francisco area to meet Don. I wanted to help him tell his story. As I sat in Don's kitchen along with his wife Corrine, he asked if I wanted to see his baseball collection. Realizing he had made history during his career with the Yankees, I quickly said "yes." Within a minute or so, Corrine lugged in a beat-up blue plastic laundry basket filled with baseballs, each protected with a thin paper covering. As I removed the paper, I could not believe what I was seeing. There were balls autographed by such legends as Babe Ruth, Lou Gehrig, Hank Aaron, Satchel Paige, Mickey Mantle, Yogi Berra, Bob Gibson, Jackie Robinson, and Roger Maris. Just touching these balls made me feel the aura of the game, from the years when these stars dominated play. Looking up at the Larsens, I said politely, "Uh, I think you might want to keep these balls in a safe or somewhere so they won't get damaged. You realize, don't you, that they are worth enough to put your son through college?" They agreed, and the money turned out to be a blessing when their son, Scott, was ready for his college days.

Together, Don and I wrote *The Perfect Yankee: The Story of the Greatest Miracle in Baseball History*. Besides a hardcover edition, the publisher released a leather-bound edition signed by Don and Yogi Berra, Don's catcher on that amazing day of October 10, 1956. Later, due to the success of the book, a trade paperback edition was released. Its cover bore the photo of Yogi jumping into Don's arms after the final out, one completed against the defending world champion Brooklyn Dodgers. Their team included such legends as Duke Snider, Roy Campanella, Jackie Robinson, Gil Hodges, Pee Wee Reese and Sal "The Barber" Maglie, who pitched against Don. The book's success was due in part to a *New York Times Book Review* accolade, which read: "Informative and entertaining."

During the following years, I also wrote an inspirational book about Cecilia Rexin, a German Christian and Holocaust survivor, entitled *Testament to Courage*. The book chronicled her years in a concentration camp where she, as an angel of mercy, saved the life of an orphaned Russian girl by entrusting a Nazi prison guard. My next book was a biography of Jack Nicklaus, one that he told me inspired his finally completing his own autobiography, which he had been working on for more than twenty years. I chose another superstar of sport, Larry Bird, as a subject for my next book, entitled *Larry Legend*. It focused on the former Boston Celtic legend's first year of coaching the Indiana Pacers. In fact, Larry was supposed to write the book with me but when an agent could not secure more than a four-hundred-thousand-dollar advance, Larry balked. I wrote the book anyway, one that showed how Larry became disenchanted with coaching players who never gave half the effort he did even though they were making millions to play the game. During that season, Larry's Pacer team reached the Western Conference Finals against the Chicago Bulls. I had a press row seat to watch Michael Jordan, Scottie Pippen and Dennis Rodman show their superstar stuff. During that game, Jordan dove through the air like a swan, his moves so deft that opposing players had little chance to guard him. His shot floated so beautifully it hit the net with an almost silent "swoosh." Watching him play with his tongue sticking out of his mouth and with a zest for precision moves others could not even dare try, I could not help but conclude that the player known as "Air Jordan" was the greatest to ever play his sport. While I was walking with the gifted writer David Halberstam after a playoff game, he told me Jordan was the "smoothest" player he had ever seen, one with a mindset that permitted him to play at a level others only dreamed about.

My books about Tyson, Larsen, Nicklaus, and Bird parlayed into appearances on *ESPN Classic*, which broadcasted biographies about these gifted athletes. Yet another book about golf, this one called *Diamonds in the Rough*, permitted me to hobnob with more superstars of old as I followed them on the senior golf tour. Meeting

Arnold Palmer, Gary Player, Chi Chi Rodriguez (who gave me a small bottle of bee's honey to cure a cold), Bob Murphy, Hale Irwin, and Jim Colbert, then the best senior player in the world, bedazzled me. "Arnie," as Palmer was called, was the same down-to-earth man he was made out to be. When I talked to him on the practice tee for a tournament he was about to begin, I noticed the reverence the other players had for the "King of Golf." When Arnie talked, people listened; he was such a fan favorite, a hard-driving player whose swashbuckling style captivated anyone who watched him play. I was most drawn to his magnetic personality. It reminded me of the same sort of aura I had experienced the day I accompanied Paul Newman in his race car for the *People* program segment. James Stewart exuded that same sort of magnetism but his was more sedate. People like Palmer and Newman simply overwhelmed others; there was power about them, a feeling of being in the presence of royalty.

One day I watched Sam Snead, at the time in his late seventies, practice sand bunker shots in 95-degree heat in Palm Springs. He had his trademark straw hat on while his nephew J. C. Snead stood nearby. When the balls dropped on the practice green, none were more than five feet from the hole. J. C. just kept shaking his head in admiration as sweat ran down Sam's cheeks. The legend was still trying to better his game despite his advanced age.

Believing that he might want to write a book about his remarkable record-setting performances on tour, Jim Colbert invited me to his home in Arizona to discuss our collaboration. Before we did so, he surprised me by asking if I wanted to play golf at nearby Big Horn. I told Jim I didn't have any clubs with me. He smiled and said, "Come with me." In his garage, beside a brand new black Cadillac he had won for being Senior Tour player of the year, rested more than twenty brand new Callaway golf bags stuffed with the latest brand new Callaway clubs. On a neighboring shelf I spotted stacks of boxes filled with brand new Callaway golf balls. Brand new Footjoy golf shoes littered the floor alongside boxes of brand new Callaway golf shirts. "Take your pick," Jim told me. "Anything you want." And I did, outfitting myself from head to toe with a new shirt, a new golf glove, new shoes that fit perfectly, new golf balls, and new clubs all around. When I plopped on a brand new Callaway golf hat, I felt like I was ready to attack any course as a true professional. I only wish that had been the case.

First, Jim suggested we hit a few balls on the practice range, but when I put the golf bag back on our cart, I failed to properly fasten it. As we headed up a slight slope on the asphalt cart path, I heard a thud and then *clang, clang, clang.* Turning around, I watched the brand new golf clubs as they scattered about when the bag fell off the cart and hit the path. When I picked up the clubs, I noticed they had black marks on the flanges. Colbert didn't say anything out of courtesy, but I felt like the "dumbhead" my dad used to call me.

Then, on the first tee, I was so nervous that my first shot, a low liner, nearly killed a poor course worker two fairways to the left of where we were playing. He ducked and then raised his rake high in the air in protest as he screamed obscenities in my direction. Colbert laughed when he walked over to me and said, "Maybe next time you should tee the ball a little higher."

Writing mostly sports books was my entry into the publishing world, but I vowed to tackle more compelling subjects. One I hoped to write involved the first man to walk on the moon, Neil Armstrong. When I met him for lunch in the Cincinnati area, his demeanor reminded me of James Stewart, and of my father, men I respected for being markedly humble despite their accomplishments. Mr. Armstrong had enjoyed a couple of the books I had written, but try as I might, I could not convince him to collaborate on his autobiography with me.

In effect, words became my tool for reflecting on the world we live in. Almost all of my books were historical in nature, providing an opportunity to make people stop and think about important issues of the day. After writing *Testament to Courage*, I considered writing a book about a religious or spiritual figure, but none came to mind. This was probably because I still only looked at this part of my life on a surface level, praying at times but never reading the Bible or becoming a regular at church. Like others, I was simply too busy, I told myself, to give God my full attention.

Always on the lookout for new challenges, and despite any experience in radio, I agreed to travel down another road by hosting a three-hour afternoon talk show in nearby Bloomington on WGCL right after Rush Limbaugh's program. We discussed local issues such as city council debates and property tax questions. When the city sought to condemn the farmland of a gentleman named Wallace Holmes for use as a fire station, I raised hell, and the mayor finally backed down. From thereon, I achieved a following, and the show became quite popular. I particularly enjoyed the segments called "Harry from Heaven." Jim Crago (J.C.), the show's engineer, did a perfect imitation of recently deceased Chicago Cubs announcer Harry Carey. The audience loved it, too, as they did another called "Mr. Hollywood" in which my friend Jeff Dellinger asked "six degrees of Kevin Bacon" trivia questions that nobody could answer.

When ESPN asked me to comment on the O. J. Simpson case the day he was driving around LA's freeways evading the police, I appeared via satellite on the Jim Rhome program and described how

Simpson's fleeing would inhibit his defense at trial. Later I commentated on the trial itself while recalling the party in LA when I had met O. J. and his wife Nicole. My prediction that he would be acquitted was met with skepticism, but my experience as a defense trial lawyer told me the prosecution's performance was dismal.

On the radio program, I bounced around many subjects, but one was always front and center: the rollercoaster world of Bob Knight, whose outlandish tactics as Indiana University's head coach were fodder for every program. I was a strong critic of his, believing that if he were any other university employee, he would have been fired long before. But Knight wasn't any other employee—instead he was the famous coach who donated enormous amounts of money to the library and other causes and graduated his players without a blemish of scandal. All this helped mask the embarrassment he caused the university with irreverent shenanigans both on and off the basketball court. The enablers in IU's hierarchy kept letting the bully get away with the tirades as his ego blasted out of control. Nobody could stop him, and even though at one point IU officials informed him in no uncertain terms to behave while imposing a "zero-tolerance" edict (one more embarrassing incident and he was out the door), everyone knew it was only a matter of time when Knight would erupt like a volcano, burning everyone in his path. Little did I know I was about to be on that path, destined to collide with the bombastic coach as the Spirit guiding my life, I realized later, had decided to use me for a special purpose.

Complicating the coach's attitude was his inability to match his earlier successes at IU where he had won three NCAA championships during the late 1980s and early 1990s. As the new decade began, he had good, not great, teams, and IU eventually disappeared during the early rounds of the NCAA tournament. Just like Hollywood types who find success, struggle to keep it, and then suffer when they lose it, Knight was tormented by his fall from stardom. When allegations surfaced in March 2000 that the coach had choked a player named Neil Reed during practice, an incident captured on videotape, he should have been fired on the spot. But the athletic director and Board of Trustees, including Knight's former lawyer, never stood up to the "General," a nickname Knight relished as a military history buff.

Unfortunately, the coach wasn't the only one whose egotistical tendencies had run rampant. I was a good guy and a good parent and husband, but my ego had skyrocketed with the publishing of the books, the television exposure, and the radio life. Somehow I had become a severe critic, judgmental beyond belief, a know-it-all self-righteous jerk who believed everyone else was wrong, and that I was right. I began to take criticism too personally, I let others upset my balance, and I did not pay enough attention to the simple things in life—my wife, the kids, the lovely home on our serene property, and the chance to write books. Instead, I told the world what I thought it needed to hear, and became too loud, too preachy, and too self-righteous for my own good. Instead of enjoying the good life, I became way too much of a "me" person with the belief that the world revolved around Mark Shaw. I was lost, both morally and spiritually, but didn't know it.

This was especially true as the radio program continued. My comments were too harsh, too explosive, too inflammatory, sometimes even hurtful, toward every public figure whether it was the Bloomington mayor, the city council, or Bob Knight. On the day the university severely reprimanded the coach for the Neil Reed incident, for berating and physically intimidating a university secretary when he yelled at her and threw a potted plant in her direction, for attacking an assistant coach for derogatory comments about the team, and for choking and punching the longtime university sports information director while refusing to even talk to the athletic director who had defended him so many times, I ranted on in a sarcastic tone for three hours. I called university officials "wimps" and made fun of their four-prong decision to fine Knight thirty thousand dollars, suspend him for three games, order a general apology, and be fair in his relations with the media. I said it was time for the coach to go, that he should have been fired immediately. Those who heard the broadcast must have felt they were listening to a raving maniac with a personal vendetta toward Knight. They were right, but I couldn't see it at the time, even though one listener called in and insightfully added that I was correct when I called myself a "a man of many talents, but too few of any."

From time to time, I noticed that my anger on the program translated to anger away from the microphone. It was little things at first, especially when things did not go my way. I was upset by trivial things, and by those in the publishing industry who didn't live up to expectations, but I was most upset when the triplets told me they were not going to attend my alma mater Purdue University as promised, but instead IU. Since I had worked behind the scenes to gain them admission to Purdue even though their grades didn't measure up, I was disappointed with their decision. I wanted them to get away from home, from their mother and me, and go out into the world where new experiences would force them to grow into themselves.

To this end, the triplets, a friend of theirs and I had traveled to California on a guys' road trip. It was a grand time all around. We rented a convertible and the five of us sang songs and hooted and hollered as we drove down the wild and crazy Sunset Strip where I had hung out years before. Then we visited the infamous Venice Beach where the bodybuilders tanned themselves. We played basketball in the sunshine with the Pacific Ocean a stone's throw away. We visited the campus of Pepperdine in Malibu. Set on a mountaintop with a breathtaking view of the ocean to the west, the school featured a business program that I believed was ideal for the triplets. I hoped they might consider attending and Chris and I could then enjoy visits when the winter winds in Indiana were blowing snow across every highway.

The decision to attend IU meant no Pepperdine and no Purdue. West Lafayette where Purdue was located wasn't that far away, but at least it wasn't a half hour away. But the triplets didn't care what I thought and I was really upset with them. I let anger dictate my feelings regarding their decision, the only real blemish on my years as a stepfather. Finally, I cooled down and helped them with their entry into IU. Together, we visited the school of business to get oriented.

The triplets' decision to head for Bloomington meant one other thing—I could not continue the radio program where I was on the air every day criticizing Coach Knight. Even though I had a different last name than they, I was concerned that some Knight loyalist might harm them in retaliation. With regret, but in the best interests of the triplets, I resigned. During the final program, I even tried to calm the waters regarding the coach by saying that I hoped Knight "shaped up," and that IU won the NCAA basketball championship that year. When I left the radio studio for the final time, I believed I had heard the last of the infamous Bobby Knight. I hadn't.

CHAPTER FIVE

The Knightmare

Of all the occupations the Good Lord guided me toward, being a radio talk show host was the most rewarding. Each day, without having to dress up—a true blessing for a fellow who disliked such things, for someone who enjoyed wearing socks of different colors and a worn Cubs hat—I ambled into a studio and conversed with people about various aspects of life. Before my ego got the best of me and I began to shout at the world in dismay, the program was quite popular. But instead of listening to callers, I used much of the program as a bully pulpit as I had now become an authority on just about everything. Instead of "The Voice of Common Sense," and "Defender of the Downtrodden"—the labels station management used for advertising—they could have called me "Mr. Smart Mouth" or "Mr. Negative," since I blasted everything in sight with sarcasm or negativity. I displayed a true lack of respect for others. When I later reflected on my war with Robert Montgomery Knight, I decided that the Spirit had decided I needed a wake-up call. Bobby Knight was simply the messenger.

In the fall of 2000, as George W. Bush and Al Gore readied themselves for the presidential election, I was completing a biography of Jonathan Pollard, the American Navy intelligence specialist who had spied for the Israelis. Meanwhile, Knight was approaching another basketball season while under the tight leash Indiana University had imposed on him. Some agreed with the zero-tolerance policy that had been imposed after the Neil Reed incident; some did not. Regardless, the coach, as mutual acquaintances had informed me, was seething with disgust at certain university officials whom he felt had betrayed him.

At the same time, my stepssons were immersed in the exciting fall events of their first year of college. Each of the triplets was ready to soak up all IU had to offer, including socializing with the beautiful young coeds who flocked to the university.

Despite reservations regarding their attending IU, I was still sad knowing that they would no longer be living at home. The triplets were gone; a new cycle of life was about to begin.

When they decided to pick up some football tickets on a chilly, clear day at Assembly Hall where IU played its basketball games, little did they know that an unlikely incident was about to catapult them from an innocuous existence as college students into a world of constant media exposure. Purely by coincidence, or so it seemed at the time, while Kent, his two brothers, and a friend were leaving (the basketball season was months away), a surly Knight walked into the complex toward them on the way to his office. According to the triplets, after Kent simply asked, "What's up, Knight?" the coach grabbed him with a grip strong enough to leave red marks on his forearm while chastising him for his lack of respect. In his loud, authoritative voice, the one that players feared, he told Kent he should be addressing him as "Mr. Knight," or "Coach Knight" and then attacked Kent with a barrage of expletives. An international audience would soon debate for months whether Kent's remarks had been disrespectful, or simply a nervous reaction when he encountered the intimidating, six-foot-five-inch, two-hundred-pound-plus coach.

My contact with Knight had been minimal before the incident. Our beloved family doctor, Dr. William Howard, a great friend, knew Knight and expressed mixed feelings about him. He respected how the coach gave back to the Bloomington community and the IU library, and helped many behind the scenes, but, like many others, he despised the coach's holier-than-thou attitude and complete disregard for decent treatment of those who questioned his authority. Despite this, at one time I had considered writing a book about or with the coach. I approached him through a mutual friend Larry, who served as the physician for the basketball team. Nothing came of it, and I moved on to other projects.

To anyone paying attention, there was no doubt Coach Knight was a disturbed man suffering from a fear of failure, which contributed to his bullying persona. His ability to win championships was in the past, and he no longer was considered among the top echelon of college coaches in the United States. Instead of being respected by most, he was merely tolerated as fewer and fewer blue chip players committed to IU. He still had his followers, his band of Knight "loyalists," but even those who worshipped him questioned whether his best days were behind him.

As I later realized when I considered my own obnoxious behavior, when a person is angry at another, it is mostly a projection of the angered party's state of mind. Any amateur psychologist would have realized Knight was wound too tight as the 2000 season approached.

Imagine, the great Bob Knight harnessed, leashed by a no-tolerance policy. What an embarrassment for a man who desperately needed counseling in the form of anger management. Ironically, so did I, but I was in denial just like he was.

On my radio show, before I had resigned, I had suggested Knight take a leave of absence, perhaps for a year or more, to soothe the frustration and anger boiling beneath the surface. But his stubborn attitude rejected such a plan, and only his wife Karen's pleas to the IU president saved him from being fired after the Neil Reed choking incident.

The triplets had met Knight just once before in their lives, the year they attended his basketball camp along with their friend Brett. During Knight's preliminary talk, he had used cuss words the triplets had never heard before. They were all turned off by the crude behavior, and lost some respect for the coach. To many, Knight was the prototypical angry man. When his name was mentioned, the first response was, "Oh, he's the one who threw the chair," or "He's the one who kicked his son Patrick," then a player, a reference to ugly incidents during games when Knight lost control.

Since Knight was a short fuse ready to be lit at any time, it was no wonder he retaliated against my stepson Kent's words, "What's up Knight?" Later, I realized that grabbing Kent had nothing to do with Kent; Coach Knight was grabbing IU and all the critics who were after him, who wanted the great coach to fail and be fired from his job. Attacking a young student who meant no harm was Knight's way of saying he was not going to take it anymore. When he chastised Kent for lack of respect, the coach was screaming at the world for its lack of respect for a man who had given his heart and soul to basketball and the university. One could sympathize with Knight; he must have been in great pain as he entered Assembly Hall on that fateful day, upset at something or somebody, allowing his unchecked temper to surface.

I was in my writing studio when I heard about the incident. My canine friends, Snickers and Peanut Butter, were snoring away when Kent called and said, "I just ran into the coach." I first thought he meant there was a traffic accident. But his voice was weaker than usual and I quickly understood that Kent was scared. Trembling, he recounted what had occurred as his brothers hovered around him, each shocked over the run-in.

When Kent asked me what to do about the incident, I violated the first rule of parenthood: the kids come first. Instead of considering how this incident might impact my stepsons, I thought of myself and my distaste for Knight. Instead of acting like a mature individual, and one who should have considered the effect that such publicity would have on the triplets, my main focus was on how reporting the incident might finally rid IU of Knight. I also am sure I thought of how my involvement might boost my own career, albeit with good intentions because I did believe that Kent was owed an apology.

My advice to Kent was that if he wanted me to, I would report the incident to Indiana University officials. Relying on me to make the right decision, he agreed, and instead of calling Coach Knight and handling the matter privately, I called Christopher Simpson, a university official. He immediately told me the IU police would be alerted, something that we should have avoided. Realizing I ought to warn Knight, I called his office, but he was not there. I left a detailed message about the incident with an assistant and asked that the coach call me back. To my regret, and I believe to his as well, he never did so.

Scrambling to understand how I could protect Kent and the triplets as the IU police handled the matter, I decided to make certain Kent and his brothers got a fair shake in the media. My instincts told me Knight would come out swinging in order to save his job by denying that he had harmed Kent, since the coach knew what the consequences of grabbing a student could be. Having worked for ESPN, I knew David Brofsky, a producer there from my Tyson trial coverage, would listen to the story and make certain it was reported in a fair manner. After I talked to him, I wondered if I had made the right choice, and upon reflection, I was sure I had. Knight tried to manipulate the media from the moment they contacted him, but reporters already had our side of the story, the truth, an important advantage that put Knight on the defensive instantly. Kent later wondered why I had given the news to ESPN, and permitted so many interviews. I understood his concern, but I was only trying to protect him and his brothers. My heart was in the right place, and I wanted to act in his best interest but my mind was clouded with thoughts of how the media attention might affect me and my career. This was a mistake on my part, one for which I would pay dearly. I should have recognized that my reporting of the incident, a violation of the zero-tolerance policy imposed on him, would cause Knight to counterattack.

Each day from then on would bring surprise and dismay at how the incident escalated in importance. Certainly my overall conduct during the affair was debatable at best. Being "media savvy," as one newspaper reporter put it, I was aware of how important it was for me to stick up for Kent and his brothers' version of what occurred. But I was a parent as well, and unfortunately, the media side of me continued to overshadow the parental side. Too often, I was selfish in savoring the attention, of being in the limelight when I should have kept my mouth shut. Some said I was too hard on myself since I did have the boy's best interest at heart, but there is no doubt I could have handled much of the media interaction better. Some nights I lay awake questioning my actions, hoping that somehow the furor would end. It didn't.

All the while, Chris trusted me to handle things. She had been quite upset with Knight's behavior once she saw the red marks on Kent's arm. Protective of the triplets, she continued to look out for their best interests, as one would expect from a loving mother.

Over the next few days, news spread at a rapid, uncontrollable pace. First, the triplets were interviewed by IU campus police in Bloomington as media photographers appeared at every angle. While at campus police headquarters, we all watched Knight hold an impromptu televised news conference where he denied any wrongdoing while calling me his most "vitriolic critic," a term I had to look up in the dictionary. But the gist of what he was saying was that as a radio show critic, I was out to get him and had used the triplets as a setup. Based on my radio show rants, who could blame him? But nothing was further from the truth. Regardless, many people, especially his loyalists, the ones who thought he was a god, believed his allegations for one basic reason: was it really possible that out of more than *forty thousand* students, Knight had grabbed *my* stepson despite his having no idea that Kent was related to me? The odds of this occurrence had to be a zillion to one. Only later would I understand how such an event was meant to be, for several reasons.

With both sides telling their version of the story to the thirsty media, the war of words persisted. People sent me hateful e-mails and telephone messages, many containing death threats. I was dubbed the "evil stepfather," and terms unprintable here. And then matters worsened. On the day when Larry, the mutual friend of ours, and I believed we had crafted an acceptable apology letter from the coach that he had basically agreed to sign, university President Myles Brand delivered the verdict: Knight was fired. The statement said that the action was taken not only because Knight had grabbed a student, but because of other reprehensible conduct involving university personnel, including an ugly incident with the IU legal counsel and what Brand called "several instances in which Knight's behavior had violated the [zero-tolerance] policy." Knight had also, according to IU, been insubordinate regarding alumni functions, and, perhaps worse in the administration's eyes, refused to meet with President Brand regarding the "Kent incident" and instead had headed for Canada on a fishing trip.

If I had known of the "several instances" of bad behavior during the previous summer months, knowledge that both the university and Knight were aware of, and that IU officials were looking for a final straw with which to fire Knight, would I have thought twice about reporting Kent's incident to IU officials? Certainly being in the dark about their intentions left me unable to consider all the ramifications, but regardless I probably would have proceeded since I really felt it was time for IU and Knight to part ways. However, I could have handled the matter better by slowing things down and collecting more information instead of forging ahead at breakneck speed.

I considered President Brand's firing of Knight hypocritical, since it was Brand who had cozied up to the coach during his time in office. When I attended an IU practice one year, I had watched as

Brand walked arm-in-arm with the coach across the court, both laughing at whatever Knight had said. At one point, Brand told someone, supposedly in jest, the only two things at the university he could not control were the parking problems and Coach Knight. In effect, the president had enabled Knight's transgressions as had most members of the university Board of Trustees, many of whom were Knight's allies and refused to call for discipline before it was too late. The "Kent incident," for whatever reason, had finally pushed even the naysayers, including his friends on the board, over the line. Knight had to go.

The moment Brand announced the firing at a news conference, Knight's players roamed around in shock. The war had escalated. I received more hateful e-mails from several Knight supporters. Knight loyalists peppered me with nasty names and accusations that I was the worst person on the face of the Earth. Here is an example:

"You sniveling bag of sh**!!!!!!! Why don't you move to Kentucky where you can live with your fellow Knight-haters and with people of the same mentality as yours. And take your stepsons with you!!!!!!!"

Thankfully, others disagreed:

"The courage you have shown to step up to this life-long bully is to be commended. I hope you and your stepsons stay safe and please remember we are all not blind followers of Knight and his people."

Tom Bowers, co-director of the Sports and Entertainment Academy at the IU Kelley School of Business, wrote:

"I can't thank you enough for what you, Kent, and your other stepsons have done to help us here at IU. I hope that Kent will understand that those who are making threats against him are cowards who will never do him physical harm although they might continue to attack him verbally. I hope that Kent decides to go to class and show these unprincipled cowards that he will not be intimidated by them."

I received other supportive e-mails from IU staff members as well. For too long, they believed, the university's superb programs in areas such as music and business had been overshadowed by the black cloud Knight held over IU on a steady basis. One who agreed was famed author George Plimpton. When I met him at a literary event, he said, "Oh, you're the guy who brought down Bobby Knight. Let me shake your hand."

On the IU campus, chaos reigned. Angry students burned an effigy of Kent as my e-mail and telephone death threats continued. One evening, matters became so serious that the county sheriff and a state policeman stayed at our home. Chris became scared for the triplets' safety and suggested a trip out of state to protect them. I felt relief when they wanted me to tag along, as I was worried that they might feel I had sacrificed them for my own personal gain. When we arrived at a Florida hotel (registered under an assumed name), the four of us played football on the beach as if we were truly on vacation. The boys' strength inspired me.

True friends Bobby and Leslie Weed (Bobby was a talented golf course designer mentored by Pete Dye) made our escape possible. During tough times, the Weeds always came through. They never judged me for my actions, but instead supported me and my family.

To his credit, Coach Knight and his wife Karen appeared at a campus rally and asked that Kent be left alone. But Knight continued to blame me for the entire mess as he would later do in a *Playboy* magazine article where he used enough foul words to leave little room for any other content. In an interview with journalist Lawrence Gobel, Knight lambasted Myles Brand, the IU Board of Trustees, Christopher Simpson (the university official I had alerted), IU Athletic Director Clarence Doninger, who had protected him for years, and me.

According to Gobel, a fight nearly broke out while he and Knight were riding in a car that coach Don Donoher, Knight's friend, was driving. Apparently the journalist asked Knight about me, and Knight's face reddened. He then chastised me for criticizing him on my radio program. When Gobel mentioned to Knight that I had publicly said I didn't think he should have been fired, the coach went ballistic. Knight's outburst went something like this (I have edited out the cuss words): "I'm not here for a ___ inquisition! And if that's what this is, then get the ___ out of here and hitchhike back home! The ___ stepfather was a ___ ___ from the word ___ go! He ___ lied and he lied and he lied! ___ I mean, this is my ___ life we're talking about. My ___ heart was ripped out by this ___ bull___."

Yes, Knight blamed me for the firing, and to some extent he was right. I couldn't resist the media frenzy and by doing so, had been used by the university for its own gain. I knew Knight was on "probation" and that any serious misbehavior would result in his dismissal. But I was blind to this, blind because I did not want to see, blind because deep inside perhaps I wanted to be the big shot that brought Bobby Knight down. Now the selfish Mark Shaw had been snared in his own trap.

Could I have prevented the Knightmare itself from happening? Or was it preordained, certain to occur, certain that the coach and I had to collide head-on with repercussions aplenty on both sides?

BOOK III

CHAPTER SIX

A Spiritual Awakening

Before the Knightmare, love abounded in our family and it felt like a bond existed between us that could not be broken. We had made it through the good times and the rough times and survived them all. We had been blessed in so many ways. If the Spirit was testing me to see if I could be a good stepfather, I believed I had passed the test.

Then our whole world exploded. Kent, Kyle, Kevin, Kimberly, and my wife Chris were caught in the middle of a fight, a war of words between Coach Knight and me, and also between Knight loyalists and me. Battle lines had been drawn, and like in any war, there would be casualties.

The immediate result was sad, but true. The loving bond of trust between Chris and me shattered and for the first time in our marriage, we exchanged hurtful words. For more than twelve years, aside from small spats that any couple experiences, we had been as one, truly in tune with each other as to how we wanted to live our lives. The children were our first priority. We were proud of them, and felt we had been good parents. Now that each had fled the nest, we planned to spend more time together doing things we wanted to do. If there were problems lurking beneath the surface, I had not seen them. Looking back, maybe I should have.

We were on the same page when the Knightmare initially happened, but as time passed Chris sensed that I was thinking more of Mark Shaw than of the family. I believed I was trying to protect the triplets, but she thought I went overboard and promoted myself in the process. She was, for the most part, right, and I was wrong, but I didn't realize it at the time. I had let the matter become way too personal and wanted to win. Most of all, I wanted Knight to apologize. I believed the triplets would be vindicated, and my actions justified.

As the Knightmare wound down, Chris and I began to really quarrel when she learned I was going to talk to CNN and CBS' *Early Show* one more time because I had to have the final word, had to keep talking when I should have disengaged. I had spoken to nearly every media outlet on the face of the earth, or so it seemed. Ego is a strange beast and I let mine get the best of me. Chris cooled down during the long travel south to Florida, but there was obvious tension between us. She was disappointed in me, and she had every right to be. There is a special love between a mother and her sons, and I had put the triplets, especially Kent, at risk. This was unforgiveable, though I had hoped she could forgive me over time because I had never consciously intended to put him, or his brothers, in harm's way.

When things settled down a bit, I encouraged the triplets to return to IU since they had done nothing wrong. I didn't want them running away, but Chris had made up her mind—they were never going back to that university. They agreed. Guilt set in as I realized the truth, that due to my selfish actions, the incident with Knight had escalated. Certainly Knight was also at fault, as was the university, but when I tried to sleep at night, all I could do was lay awake wondering how I had messed up so badly.

The question now was where the triplets could continue their college educations. After some discussion, I contacted my friend, Indiana University/Purdue University at Indianapolis [IUPUI] chancellor Jerry Bepko, and he immediately helped with admission requirements. The triplets enrolled there, and I relaxed for the first time in months. They enjoyed being back in college, but then an IUPUI professor became quite upset with the triplets over a mix-up with a required paper. He was so upset he felt dismissal was in order and threatened to request the university's approval. I jumped to the triplet's defense and my help with providing a logical explanation for the misconception permitted them to remain in school. This allowed me a degree of redemption, some easing of the guilt I felt for having caused the calamity in their lives. I was so grateful that I had a second chance to be the loving stepfather I had been before the Knightmare.

During visits to our home after the triplets moved to Indianapolis to attend IUPUI, I was heartened to see my bond with them restored. I must have apologized a hundred times and they appeared to understand my good intentions in protecting them.

If the relationship with the triplets was on the mend, the distance between my wife and me was widening as the days passed. I was frustrated when few people in the entertainment world wanted to be around Mark Shaw, "the man who got Bobby Knight fired," as I was now known throughout the media. I began to feel ostracized, alienated from the world, with the dogs as my only true friends. One day I was a respected author, television and radio personality, husband and parent, and the next day I was the publicity hound, the "evil" stepfather, as Knight had branded me, with a black mark x'd across my face. Some had applauded me for standing up to Knight, but despite his being fired, he was the winner and I was the loser in my mind because my marriage was on the rocks and my wife wouldn't allow the triplets to return to IU despite their having the right to do so.

I'm no marriage counselor, but when two people lose trust in each other, the relationship is usually doomed. Instead of crisis bringing Chris and me closer together, we moved further apart and could no longer communicate openly. Worried about the uncertainty of our relationship, I decided a solo road trip was in order, a cross-country adventure to California via Minnesota where the publisher of my new book, *Miscarriage of Justice*, about the spy, Jonathan Pollard, was located.

Chris agreed with the trip idea, but I could tell she was hurt that I didn't ask her to join me. She was even more disappointed in me when I did not telephone regularly.

During the drive through Wisconsin, Minnesota, South Dakota, Wyoming, Idaho, Nevada, and on to San Francisco, I listened to radio music with the truck windows down and tried to make sense of my station in life. I knew a Father's Day was looming in the distance, and that it would be a tough one for me, as I felt I had failed as a stepfather, a fill-in father. The triplets had seemed to forgive me, but I knew Chris had not. To her, I was a loser. I had failed to protect her boys.

Whatever I was looking for on the West Coast, as I traveled through San Francisco and then LA, was not there. The thought that it was time to leave the Midwest again crossed my mind. But I hated the idea of giving up on my marriage, and my relationship with the stepchildren. I was not going to be a quitter; I was not going to let Knight win by having my family life completely fall apart. Certainly the support of Jerry, the children's father, Chris' family, and my own, had meant a great deal to me. I wanted to show them, Chris, and my stepchildren that I was never going to leave.

After a morning sitting and listening to the waves of the Pacific Ocean hit the beaches near Malibu, I decided to return to Indiana. Attempting to patch things up with Chris, I suggested meeting in Las Vegas. Kimberly, who had fled Indiana for a new adventure, was living there. The three of us shared a grand time together visiting a casino and celebrating her birthday. When Kimberly gave me a big hug, it meant the world to me.

Chris and I then headed for the mystical town of Sedona, Arizona. Standing in the Chapel of the Holy Cross, built on a twin-pinnacled spur about 250 feet high, jutting out of a thousand-foot red rock wall, a rock the church promotes as solid as the Rock of Peter, over-whelmed us. I sat in one of the pews and said a silent prayer hoping that our relationship might improve, that we might rediscover the love we once knew. Asking the Spirit for this blessing seemed unfair after how I had conducted myself, but I asked anyway.

Before leaving, we also dined beside a river where the soothing sounds of the rushing water provided quiet time to talk about what lay ahead. During the cross-country trip home, we tried to sort out what was separating us, what was causing the tension we both felt. Could we reconcile the hurt she had experienced through the Knightmare? I wondered during the long stretches of highway as we crossed the Mississippi River toward Indiana.

When we arrived home, I thought the marriage could be saved. For a time I believe we both acted like it could. But Chris no longer trusted me. Little things turned into big things, and we were more strangers than loving husband and wife.

Realizing how unhappy Chris was, I considered leaving myself, but I did not want to put the children through another divorce. Regardless, Chris decided I was too ragged to stand anymore, especially when I acted like an idiot feeling extremely sorry for myself. We tried to fix the marriage with the help of a counselor, but our end was nearing. Even small incidents of disagreement turned into mountains of conflict. I withdrew into a shell where I did not listen to the cautionary words that Chris was clearly communicating to me as she wrestled with her own demons. Finally, one morning, it was apparent the marriage was over. The Knightmare had two more victims: a couple who had dearly loved each other and shared the joy of raising four terrific children.

When I sat on a bench overlooking our pond, my hands trembled and I felt extremely cold even though it was a hot day. I had bloodshot eyes from too little sleep, pondering how I had blown it, had screwed up royally in so many ways. When two people who have spent more than a decade together split, the blame goes both ways, but the temptation to "get" Bobby Knight while becoming a big shot had been too much for me. Now I would no longer be a stepfather, no longer be a part of a wonderful family. I would be alone, again.

A few days later I left our home for the final time, saddened at the turn of events. Soon afterwards, I was sitting in a lawn chair in front of a cottage a hundred yards from Princess Lake, a half-hour drive from Nashville. My niece Shari and her husband Mitch had lovingly offered it to me. My only companion was now Black Sox, the puppy that Chris' sister had given to us before the breakup.

As a few clouds floated by on an otherwise clear, blue-sky day, a million thoughts came to mind. I was hurt. I was disappointed. I felt like a failure. I was confused, and I was afraid—afraid of the uncertainty that lay ahead. There were many stressful days and nights, ones where I slept few hours worrying about many things— what friends, and people in general, would think; how those who hated me would revel in the news; how Bob Knight might feel knowing I had lost my marriage; how my own family would feel over news of the breakup. *Poor Mark, poor Mark,* I kept thinking. *How could this happen to you?* And the children. How I had let them down, failed them. Now they would go through yet another divorce, one I hoped would not be as bitter as the previous one they had experienced. I would make sure of that. Chris and I would reach a quick settlement, and then go on with our separate lives. The kids would still be close to me and we would spend time together and resurrect the closeness we once knew. *Everything will work out,* I thought, trying to convince myself that I could make my plan a reality.

During times of darkness and grief, I cried out for help trying to make sense of how our marriage had failed. Suddenly, I felt abandoned, an emotion I truly never quite understood until years later when the miracle occurred. These feelings stretched beyond family to friends who suddenly wanted nothing to do with me. One friend, a diehard Knight supporter whose whole life revolved around "The General," had greeted me at the local post office by saying, "Well, you finally got him, didn't you?" I had no idea how to respond. I was sure Knight was still as confounded as I, that out of forty thousand students, he had grabbed *my* stepson. Only later would all this make sense; only later would I realize why I had to experience the Knightmare.

Certainly there were friends who stood by me during the Knightmare. Jerry Bales, Rudy Crabtree, Kermit Flynn, and Sheriff Dave Anderson defended me to anyone who would listen. But one close friend, another Knight supporter, yelled at me when I called him. Even after I apologized, he refused an offer to meet and talk things over. He never spoke to me again, something I truly regret.

Fortunately, from the moment of separation through the perplexing months of 2002 and 2003, I had a friend, a new friend that would see me through the darkest days. Over the years, I had used every excuse known for not reading the Bible: it was too tough to read; it would take too long; I could never understand it; it was too religious; it was only for those who wanted to study it. I knew all the excuses and they were my excuses. Easy crutches to lean on.

Before my marriage breakup, I had noticed Kevin reading a study Bible. It had commentary alongside the biblical text as sort of a "cheat sheet" to understanding the meaning of God's word. Impressed, I glanced over Kevin's shoulder, and asked him if he would give me one like his as a Christmas gift. He did.

When Chris and I separated, and I didn't know where to turn, I opened the black book with my name imprinted on the front and was immediately drawn to the Book of James. As I read, I began to understand how it wasn't "if" problems were going to transpire in one's life, it was just a matter of "when." With this insight, things began to make more sense to me in a spiritual way. James soon became my new best friend as I read, and read, and read some more each day. I was especially comforted on the first Father's Day apart from the stepchildren.

I scoured the Bible and discovered new points of interest that really made sense as I encountered daily pain with the pending divorce. I began scribbling notes in red ink in the margins as I went along, things to think about and remember as I lamented the end of our relationship. Lonelier now than ever, the book was my only salvation. On many nights, my empty stomach growled in protest as I wrestled with disappointment, confusion, and fear of the future. Certainly the big-shot Mark Shaw had been cut down to size.

Each day, I read from the study Bible and learned new ways of understanding what God was putting me through. Indeed, He had knocked me over the head with a sledgehammer and then a jack-hammer. He had decided to wake me up and make me realize that my life was empty without Him, without any guiding Spirit to carry me along. I thought, "Yeah, this makes sense. Let's learn more."

I was particularly drawn to the book of Job 6:2 where it is written: "Then Job replied, 'If only my anguish could be weighed, and all my misery be placed on scales! It would surely outweigh the sand of the seas—no wonder all of my words have been impetuous. The arrows of the Almighty are in me. My spirit drinks of their poison. God's terrors are marshaled against me.'" That was how I felt, that God's arrows, those alerting me to the realization that I had wronged in His eyes, were sticking in every part of my body and soul. How to remove those arrows became my quest. If Job, who had lost everything—his wealth, his family, his health—could do it, so could I.

The Spirit now guiding me assisted once again with my journey when it directed me to a Borders bookstore on the south side of Indianapolis one sunny afternoon. While browsing indiscriminately, I spotted a table full of books across the room. As if a magnet drew me there, I walked over for a closer look. Stacked high was a purple-covered book called *The Purpose Driven Life*, by Pastor Rick

Warren, the conservative evangelist and senior pastor at California's Saddleback Church, the eighth largest in the United States. The book had catapulted Rev. Warren to international fame with more than forty million copies sold.

As I stood before the stacks of books, it felt as if the Spirit were directing my hand to pick up one. The moment I did and read a few words on the inside cover jacket, I knew the Spirit wanted me to purchase the book and read it. From the very first four words, "It's not about you," I knew God was about to open a whole new life for me, one filled with His direction through His word and His path.

Each morning, after Black Sox and I took a walk, I read a new section (the book is divided into forty sections that one can read easily in fifteen minutes). From that moment on, this became my daily ritual. I read and then prayed so that my mind would be focused on being Christlike in everything that I did during every single second of the day. My mantra became: "Every thought, every action— Christlike." One great lesson to be learned from the book was Rev. Warren's suggestion that to rekindle broken relationships, a person should apologize even if he or she did not feel they had done anything wrong. This lesson came in handy as the years passed.

During the tough times of dealing with the divorce, I was able to rely on the book and on God to see me through. Soon Jesus, part of the most wondrous Father/Son relationship in the history of mankind, was my best friend alongside John and Job and all of the biblical characters. They became inspirations to me as I tried to make it through the day. At night when I fell asleep with Black Sox nearby, I knew God loved me and wanted the best for me. But, at the same time, I knew there would be difficult times ahead that I would have to endure.

Through the summer of 2003, I experienced a kind of inner peace with a Higher Power to lean on; the Good Lord became an armor of sorts. I realized that nothing else mattered except what He and the Spirit thought of my words and actions. Some days, I would sit alone with only the wind as company and ask, "Lord, how am I doing?" to check on my progress. This didn't mean I could always overcome the temptation to lash out when disgusted with how I was being treated. I was still learning how to handle anger when I felt wronged or misunderstood.

I fought hard to control my emotions, but sometimes I failed. Each day, I learned more about trusting God with the power of prayer and asking Him to guide me. Slowly, I was becoming a decent human being again, with the Spirit, this mysterious Higher Power, as the foundation of my life.

With this wonderful learning process in full swing, I was changing daily, even minute by minute, as I accepted the incredible lessons God was teaching me. A whole new world was opening up, one I had never encountered before. I had been awakened, awakened to the understanding that I could not live without some sort of Spirit leading me in the right direction. Otherwise I knew, truly knew, I was doomed to endless failure.

During the fall of 2003, the war of words during the divorce heightened. The hurt and pain I endured would have knocked me over just months earlier, but I was able to withstand the barrage because God was there for me. I had finally realized a most important point—that God presents us with problems not to punish us but to test us, to educate us, and make us stronger, which prevented me from striking back, and permitted me forgiveness and love in taking the high road, the Christian road that God had led me down when I was so in need of His guidance. When I reflected on Bobby Knight, I began the process of forgiveness as I hoped he might do the same.

In effect, I was being transformed, and through the heartache, I was becoming stronger and more Christlike every day in my words and my actions. Each day, I would pray: "Lord, fill me with the Holy Spirit and let me be Christlike in everything I do." This new mindset was working as I continued on the path He had paved for me.

One of the graces God provided was the continued support of my immediate family, one I had neglected for years when I bonded with Chris, my stepchildren, and Chris' family. I rarely saw either my brother Jack and his wife Sue, or sister Debbie, and even though Anne lived close by, I spent little time with her. But when the crisis erupted, both the Knightmare and the marriage breakup, they were all there for me. If I had stayed married, I might never have reunited with my brother and sisters, which made me think considerably about what the Spirit, this indefinable, yet definable, "something" leading me along, had in store for me. I was consumed by wonder and the spiritual journey, one leading toward a miracle, hadn't even begun in earnest yet.

When the Spirit is at work in our lives, events that once seemed unrelated to our lives often prove otherwise. In July 2003, after spending that very lonely Father's Day inspired by more readings of James and Job, I learned about Los Angeles Lakers basketball superstar Kobe Bryant's ordeal near Eagle, Colorado, a half hour or so west of Vail, when he was charged with sexual assault. The young woman in question was an employee in a swanky hotel. The case had made international headlines.

I noted the incident like most everyone else did, not paying too much attention to it until one day when my telephone rang. My friend David, the producer at ESPN, was calling; not only did he want me as the legal analyst for the Bryant case, but as the chief legal analyst for the network. I was blown away with such an invitation; I thought that perhaps it might resume my television career. But the next day, the blessing was revoked when David told me that corporate politics had shunned me in favor of a more well-known analyst. Permitting old feelings to creep back into my psyche, I almost let my anger get the best of me. The old Mark Shaw would have lashed out, called my friend and yelled about how he had let me down, blaming everyone in my path for the slight.

With my new Christlike mindset in tow, I exercised patience, a virtue I had been working on for some time. As I walked along the shore at Princess Lake, a new outlook permitted me to consider the *why*s behind the decision, and I dismissed the disappointment as not being in God's favor. My spiritual growth allowed me insight into God's ways: many times the things we want are not good for us, and the Good Lord has something even better in mind for us.

The Bryant case still interested me as a book project, and so I decided to travel to Eagle, a tiny mountain town that had not asked for, nor wanted, the infamous publicity of the Bryant case. After I had attended one hearing, the court scheduled another one for a few weeks later. Even though I was paying my own expenses, I decided I would return and attend the upcoming hearing as well.

As the time neared to leave again for Colorado, I made arrangements for Black Sox to visit his favorite kennel in Indiana. But on a late

Saturday afternoon when I was sitting down by the lake, I suddenly felt what seemed to be a tap on the shoulder, a strange feeling like none I had ever experienced. Looking around me, there was no one in sight.

At the same time, a quiet voice said, "Drive, Mark, drive." Resisting the impulse to dismiss this as some sort of weird, metaphysical experience, I looked around again but nobody was there. Then I heard the voice again, "Drive, Mark, drive." Feeling that somehow the Holy Spirit was communicating with me, I decided to heed what I somehow knew was God's voice. After calling the kennel to cancel Black Sox's reservation, I loaded bags into our old, black Chevy truck early Sunday morning, and said good-bye to my sister Anne. Black Sox and I were about to embark on a cross-country road trip to Eagle.

During the two-day trip, I listened to the plain-talking television evangelist Reverend Charles Stanley's spiritual tapes; they kept me company as I drove long patches of highway in hopes of clearing my mind and ruminating. For some time, I had considered leaving Indiana for a fresh start. But if I left, where was I going to live? Perhaps in Chattanooga, Tennessee where my friend and mentor Jack Lupton lived? Or perhaps Chicago, a city I loved where there might be more opportunities? Maybe California—Los Angeles or San Francisco, two of my favorite cities. Uncertainty abounded, although when I prayed, I felt God was listening and guiding me like never before. In fact, I could almost feel the Holy Spirit infiltrating my body. I was experiencing a true transformation, a mind makeover of sorts, with every second, every minute, every hour, and every day. I never discussed my so-called epiphany by the lake when I felt something touch me on the shoulder and say "Drive, Mark, drive" to anyone. I knew people would think I was crazy.

As I considered these alternatives with Black Sox asleep on my lap, I continued to ponder the principles outlined in *The Purpose*

Driven Life. Pastor Warren preached that it was important to turn over all of one's decision-making processes and problems to the Good Lord and let Him decide what was best. I was reluctant to do so, having always wanted to control everything. But I had ignored the Lord's teachings for so long that I was too stubborn to let go, not knowing what was ahead of me. In effect, fear had gripped me and I feared the unknown, as all of us do at one time or another.

The more I listened to Charles Stanley and read *The Purpose Driven Life,* the more I knew that I was really in the throes of God's plan. But was there a God, I sometimes wondered, or was that simply a convenient word to use? To me, God, The Good Lord, even Jesus Christ, were all part of a Spirit that was guiding my life, a confusing but almost irrelevant notion at the time. What I needed to do was completely surrender all of my problems over to this Spirit, and let it lead me on my path. As it says in *The Purpose Driven Life,* "Pray more and quit trying so hard." And I did pray, more intently than ever before.

When Black Sox and I arrived in Eagle, he immediately became the "media dog" for the case. He was popular with all the reporters, and their colleagues played with him and gave him water and treats. I attended another hearing for the case, one that had many subplots besides Kobe Bryant's guilt or innocence. ESPN asked me to guest commentate and I appeared on several shows. But with little hesitance, the old critical, judgmental, combative Mark Shaw emerged, apropos for most television personalities. Even though I disliked that evil person, I still had not destroyed him. When I returned to my hotel, I was ashamed of my behavior, and while praying, apologized to the Lord for backsliding. I knew the only way to quit was never to appear again on any program where that sort of behavior was tolerated.

At the close of the hearing, the judge surprised everyone by continuing the proceedings for another week. Immediately I realized that if I had flown, I would have had to fly back to take care of Black Sox. But since I had driven, he and I were free to travel wherever we wanted. As if the Spirit were speaking to me directly, I knew that my next destination would be the small mountain town of Aspen where I had spent some of the most wonderful years of my life.

CHAPTER SEVEN

Aspen II

From the moment Black Sox and I entered Aspen's city limits, I knew the Good Lord had guided me in the right direction.

Familiar landmarks abounded as I drove into town: there was the Hotel Jerome bar where I tried to interview Hunter Thompson in the 1970s and where Jack Nicholson had performed the famous scene from *Five Easy Pieces*; and the Pitkin County Courthouse where Claudine Longet had her trial and the notorious serial killer Ted Bundy had escaped by jumping from a third-floor window one afternoon in the mid-'70s after a court hearing. When news spread of Bundy going missing, a neighbor of mine in the Oklahoma Flats section of town put on his gun belt complete with a loaded pistol and *nothing else* as he mowed the lawn. He was ready to shoot Bundy straight through the heart, or scare him to death with nudity. Despite his reputation as a killer, those with a sick sense of humor printed T-shirts with Bundy's image on the front. The text read "Ted Bundy Is A One-Night Stand." At several watering holes, customers could order a "Bundy cocktail" or a "Bundy Burger," a sandwich with nothing inside the bun. Crazy times, that's for sure, ones that included a wacky Fourth of July parade that showcased every variation of human behavior.

Somehow being back in the magical little former mining town and its surrounding majestic mountains felt right, and I knew the Spirit had sent me to this wondrous place. Within hours of seeing old friends and meeting new ones, I knew Mark Shaw was moving West, *again.*

Relocating for what seemed like the five-hundredth time in my life, I called Dave Danforth, the friend with whom I had started the *Daily News* in 1978. After telling him about my plans, he offered to let Black Sox and me share his house, one that he sparingly used while operating other newspapers in California. God was truly working in my life and making my move to the Rocky Mountains possible.

On December 1, 2004, after driving to Indiana to collect our modest belongings and pack them into our black Chevy truck, Black Sox and I began the sojourn back across Indiana, Illinois, Missouri, Kansas, and the plains of Colorado to our Aspen home. A new start had begun, one directly controlled by the Good Lord. Alongside me was the study Bible and *The Purpose Driven Life.*

Within days of settling in, and after renewing friendships with those I had known in Aspen before such as Paula Zurcher, a wise woman beyond her years, I searched for a church based on the teachings in Rick Warren's book. There were several to choose from, among them the Aspen Community United Methodist Church, a church more than one hundred years old located near the historic Hotel Jerome. Somehow I was drawn to that church, perhaps because I had grown up as a Methodist in my small Indiana town. When I attended a Sunday service, the church had the right feel to it—cozy and warm with a beautiful organ and stained glass windows that let in just the right amount of sunlight. The pews were polished brown, the carpet red, and the high ceilings spacious. While listening to Pastor Richard, a theater buff, I felt a special calm. "This is my new home," I thought.

Even though attendance was minimal with sometimes as few as ten parishioners in the pews, I kept attending. When I asked a member of the board of trustees about the lack of support, he responded, "We've been trying to figure that out, too." Disappointed, I attended two other churches, but was drawn back to the Methodists. Finally I decided to visit Pastor Richard and tell him what was in my heart. I described my spiritual journey and told him I wanted to attend his church but wondered if I might get involved in the worship service by helping out. He said he was in need of a liturgist, and would welcome the assistance. The next Sunday, I stood behind the second pulpit reading announcements, presenting readings, and reading the scripture before the sermon, something I could not have imagined doing months before.

For the first time, I really felt like I was part of a church and hoped my efforts might make it grow. When I first accepted the liturgist position, I was more nervous than I had ever been during any of my television show appearances. I prayed for guidance and felt close to the Lord as I read from the Bible. With His guidance, I made it through. One Sunday, a heavy snowfall prohibited Richard from leaving his home. I took over his pastoral duties, and even delivered a sermon based on appropriate scripture. While meandering down the trail by the Roaring Fork River, I laughed when I thought of what people who knew me might think of my being a minister, even if it was for just one day.

Within weeks, I suggested to Richard that I hold meetings for a new *Purpose Driven Life* group. My intent was to lure people into the blessed sanctuary with the hope that they would become involved in the church. I advertised the first meeting through flyers and in the *Aspen Daily News* and was amazed when more than fifteen people showed up. I thoroughly enjoyed leading the group even though I was not a biblical scholar like others in the group.

Sitting on the steps leading up to the cross and the pulpits was spiritually rewarding. I listened to Aspenites of every age and social background pour out their woes in search of spiritual guidance. Aspen is considered a paradise by many with its glamour and glitter, wealth, and incredible beauty, but others have trouble finding any sense of true identity there, and suffer from loneliness and lack of meaning. As word spread of our group, people began showing up in large numbers, which made room for great discussions inspired by Rev. Warren's guideposts. Not all, including me, agreed with everything Warren had to say, but we were all touched by his book in our own ways.

Each person attending the Monday night sessions, including several single mothers and a couple of fathers estranged from their sons, received a free, hardcover copy of *The Purpose Driven Life*. This was my way of giving, of attempting to help those requiring spiritual direction.

I eventually became an official member of the church and joined the administrative council, a small group that had for years been the ruling body of the church. Meeting with them, I began to understand why church attendance had disintegrated—this was a church without a true congregation. The members (less than fifty) were mostly visitors who never participated in church matters. I believed that God had brought me to Aspen to work in this church to see if I could help in any way. I was convinced that He truly had a plan for me, one that would open up a whole new world, that of being a real missionary, a lay minister, someone who could influence and make a difference in a church that was, for all practical purposes, dead. I was open to change and I welcomed it, but I also wanted to understand *why* things were happening, and discover the true meaning behind my recent opportunities.

Outfitted with what I believed to be a "calling" to help this church, I forged ahead but soon became embroiled in the political conflicts within the organization. I meant well, but no one wanted to make any changes even though the minister was better known in town as an actor than a minister. The old, cynical Mark Shaw with his caustic tongue reemerged. Soon enough, no one wanted to hear about my visions of a new beginning for the church. I was extremely disappointed, but later understood that change comes slowly, especially to those who never want to relinquish control. No matter, being involved in this church was a significant step in my spiritual journey and I learned much from it. Perhaps one day, I thought, I might consider being a minister. Was that even possible?

Thankfully, I uncovered a true bright light when I learned a woman I knew through a friend was a struggling single mother. After her young son Eddie, age ten or so, showed up one day at her salon after school, I asked whether he might enjoy having a big brother. The next week I picked him up after school and we went to a movie. I soon helped with his enrollment in a young person's art class downvalley from Aspen. We also had some fun pretending that horses were dinosaurs, that cows were camels, and that sheep were rhinos. One day, we decided he had X-ray vision and could see through the mountains and spy on people. Being with Eddie reminded me of how much I missed and loved my stepsons and stepdaughter.

While I had been focused on helping the church and enjoying time with Eddie, the Good Lord continued to test my new faith by presenting more obstacles for me to overcome. The divorce seemed to have no end as the bickering continued.

My heart was still quite heavy from the acrimony, and if not for the Bible, *The Purpose Driven Life*, Black Sox, and the support of my family and friends, I don't know what I would have done. With God constantly by my side, I was no longer alone, and yet I still felt heavy-hearted, lost and confused on many days.

When matters looked as if they could not get worse, they did. I received the e-mail informing me that my stepchildren had decided to cut off communication with me, and my pain turned into torment. I obsessed over memories of our wonderful times together. When the triplets were little, they slept with Chris and me, two at the end of the bed and one in between us. On nights when they slept in their own beds, I tucked them in while pulling the sheets up over their heads to make them laugh. Their laughter was my favorite sound of all.

When it became time for them to drive, I taught them in an old truck we had called "Big Blue." Over time, that truck finally died of too many dents and old age, but we had lots of fun while they tried to figure out how to drive a stick shift. When our youth basketball team won a tournament, they gave me hugs that made tears roll down my cheeks. I remembered when we tried to make baseball bats out of purchased wood, but the bats turned out too square; no matter—just being with the triplets was special. Sharing with them was what life had been all about, and now it was over.

Kimberly had certainly been closer with her mother and father, but I couldn't help but think of her when a friend brought his young daughter along to lunch with me at an Aspen restaurant. As she sat on his lap, I remembered when Kimberly had sat on mine while doing some homework. When Kimberly smiled, my face lit up; it had not been easy growing up alongside triplet brothers who received considerably more attention than she did. But she never griped about it. When the house was filled with kids for sleepovers or parties, Kimberly was the big sister who watched over the triplets. She was quite protective of them despite their teasing her as little brothers do.

Finally, after breaking down and having another good cry, I turned once again to *The Purpose Driven Life* and my study Bible. I began to realize that there was nothing I could do to alter the situation and that I must have faith in God because He had a reason for His actions. I also realized Kimberly and the triplets were in a difficult spot, with their natural mother pitted against their step-father. I had to understand their predicament, and have faith that they still loved me. I knew that Chris was angry at me as she had every right to be. I had let her down; I had let everyone down. The Knightmare had crushed me and I still had not recovered. Would I ever, I wondered?

In *The Purpose Driven Life*, I clung to the phrase: "Don't let the evil acts of others let you lose your Spiritual balance." I didn't believe anyone had actually been evil, but I wrote these words on a notecard and posted them on the steering wheel of the truck to remind me that, while I could do nothing about the messy divorce or the loss of contact with the triplets and Kimberly, I could do something about how I was handling this awful turn of events. I continued to take the high road, distraught over the circumstances, but determined to permit my new faith to see me through. Praying daily about the divorce kept me sane as I awaited some sort of miraculous breakthrough.

The Good Lord was testing me, I knew this for sure, but could I handle the test?

Instead of matters improving, they worsened again. During a court hearing attended by my family members, Chris' lawyer, a good friend of mine, was tough on me as expected. I left the courtroom in a daze wondering how I had ever ended up in such a situation. But after some thought, reflection, and prayer, I believed that Chris was fearful of what lay ahead, the uncertainty of being on her own again. Like me, she was suffering and I forgave her even more because I knew she was scared, scared like me and unable to recall the special love we had known for more than a decade. I reminisced about the day I had asked her to marry me at French Lick, an Indiana resort; hiding Easter eggs; watching the kids cheer at the World Series; the fun we had at the *Diving In* movie premiere; and our wonderful trip to Cinque Terre, the five mystical villages along the Italian Riviera. When people experience a divorce, they somehow forget the good times and the special moments they shared, as if they had never happened. But such wonderful memories can actually help with realizing the blessings once granted, instead of triggering heartache.

As the days passed, I struggled with envisioning what the plan God had in mind for me looked like until I took a trip to Chattanooga to see Jack Lupton, the beloved philanthropist and true mentor whom I had met through my dear friend Jack Leer. Through a substantial financial donation, Mr. Lupton had helped me create Books For Life Foundation, a supportive organization for aspiring writers. The idea had come to me after the Knightmare when I decided I wanted to help others instead of thinking so much about myself. When I told Mr. Lupton about my dream of establishing a writer's foundation, the philanthropist with a sharp-edged tongue laughed but gave the go-ahead. He appreciated my strange sense of humor, one similar to his, and we exchanged letters—mine wordy, his usually a line or less using his favorite word, one unmentionable here. During the Foundation's life, I wrote five books about writing and the publishing process including *Book Report*, *Grammar Report*, and *Self-Publishing Report*, while conducting "How to Become a Published Author" seminars across the country and in France.

Mr. Lupton never wanted any accolades for his giving. Like James Stewart and Neil Armstrong, he was a humble man content with knowing he had made a difference in people's lives. Singlehandedly, he had renovated downtown Chattanooga, including the development of a freshwater aquarium second to none in the United States.

Before visiting Mr. Lupton on a cool, wet afternoon, I walked into a busy mall to pick up a new pocket watch. Then I bought a ticket to see a film. But as the movie began, I somehow knew that I was not supposed to be there. There was no voice telling me so, but I "felt" it, really felt something urging me to leave. Immediately, I left for the cabin I was staying in on the site of The Honors, a golf course Mr. Lupton owned. Little did I know that another defining moment was about to ensue, one nearly comparable in terms of its impact to the day I heard "Drive, Mark, drive."

One minute after walking inside, I felt compelled to turn on the television set. Any number of programs could have appeared on the screen, but there before my widening eyes was none other than Rev. Charles Stanley. Instantly believing this was another one of the "ah-ha" moments I had been experiencing since my spiritual journey began, I began to watch and listen.

Rev. Stanley's sermon described people experiencing severe problems that seem impossible to resolve. At his first words, I realized that he was speaking directly to me and my situation, because at that time I saw no hope, no apparent end in sight to the messy divorce. After a pause to glance at his Bible, he said, "When our backs are to the wall, when we see no hope, we ask the wrong question, 'Lord, what am *I* going to do?'" Instead, Rev. Stanley said, we should be asking, "Lord, what are *You* going to do using me?"

As I sat back in my chair astounded at how the Holy Spirit had lifted me out of the theater and into the cabin where I could hear this sermon, my brain immediately comprehended the impact of Rev. Stanley's message. Standing up with new resolve, I said, "Yes, this is the truth; this is the way. I must ask, 'Lord, what are You going to do using me so as to deal with this problem, this divorce, since it is up to You how this problem is going to be solved?'"

With these thoughts in mind, I kneeled, bowed my head, and prayed aloud, saying, "Alright, Lord, I am turning all this over to you since I cannot figure out how to handle it. I surrender my divorce over to you and will accept whatever you decide to do."

Fortified with hope during my time of uncertainty, I returned to Aspen, prayed about my mess, and then took action. I fired my lawyer, communicated in a civil manner with Chris' attorney, and attempted a settlement. Shortly thereafter, the Spirit brought two good friends to Aspen to see me: Pat Riley, a fellow law student who had become a well-respected appellate court judge, and Mary Beth Ramey, a top-notch trial lawyer with a reputation for getting things done. I hired Mary Beth and she assisted me with an upcoming mediation. Within a month after the life-altering experience in the cabin in Chattanooga, the divorce was over. Ironically, the final settlement was close to what I had offered as a compromise months earlier.

God had blessed me and proven that He would work in my life if I was willing to turn everything over to Him. For days, I walked around in awe at how the Good Lord had blessed me. Every morning in my prayers, I thanked Him for showing me that if I was willing to surrender the toughest issue in my life to Him, He would help me in His time, not mine. I was very blessed for I had been shown the Light. Now it was time to become even more of His missionary, His minister—to spread the word to anyone I could find about how His grace could provide enlightenment, and true peace of mind.

The next time I saw Eddie, my "little brother," I was a new man. When Father's Day rolled around, he and I spent some time together. He never knew what that meant to me, but I had regained my hope and belief that one day I might love and cherish and be a father to my own son or daughter. At age fifty-nine, I knew this was probably a long shot, but anything was possible, I told myself. Anything.

Freedom is something we many times take for granted, but with the divorce over, I felt truly free for the first time in a long time. As Black Sox and I walked on the Roaring Fork Trail one morning as other dogs romped in the river, I was at peace. Suddenly I felt more proud of the days I had spent with the stepchildren, suddenly I was able to appreciate our times together more fully. I had accepted failure with many things in my life, but I now honored my times spent as a parent. While glancing at the dancing leaves on a nearby aspen tree, I shouted, "Thank you, Lord" in a voice so loud it probably could be heard a mile away. But I was so thankful, so very thankful, for whatever Spirit was guiding me along, because it had guided me to a state of grace, one unlike any I had ever known in my life. I was in effect preparing myself to accept all the blessings that would enter my path from this point onwards, including, I would discover, a true miracle.

CHAPTER EIGHT

Seminary and Thomas Merton

For a miracle, a true miracle like no other, to occur, we must be open to the unexpected, the unknown, the unbelievable. Slowly, through a series of fortuitous experiences, I had become a better person, but I still had more work to do before I was ready to embrace my miracle.

As the days passed, I continued to remember Pastor Rick Warren's words in *The Purpose Driven Life*: "We are all ministers." This is true, he explained, regardless of whether we are formally trained.

Each and every day, if we ask for it, the Good Lord will bring people into our lives for us to help. They may appear without warning, popping up in the strangest places, and at the most astonishing times.

To keep my mind focused on ministering others, I began printing inspirational words on the inside of my hand, including "Christlike," "Faith," "Love," "Patience," "Help Others," and "Blessings." People sometimes looked at me skeptically when they saw the ink markings, but I had caught their eye and took the opportunity to speak with them about my spiritual journey, or what challenges they might be facing. I gave them a mini-hardcover copy of *The Purpose Driven Life*, which provided abridged words of encouragement based on the best seller. At one point, I noticed that I had purchased more than two hundred copies of the little book. I carried two or three with me at all times.

Most times, I simply listened to personal tales of woe. If possible, I offered words of encouragement because I believed that Christlike behavior, whether one believed in Christ or not (I never forgot my mother telling me to respect those who were nonbelievers), was the key to any spiritual transformation. This conduct, I suggested, included thoughts of love, forgiveness, non-judgmental conduct, giving, and peaceful interactions. It also meant thinking of others before myself, patience, consideration, observation, and attention. When faced with a tough problem or decision, I repeated what Charles Stanley had said about asking God what he was going to do using me as well as asking the question, "What would Jesus do?"—a simple but powerful barometer for every decision, every choice, we have to make.

As I continued walking the trails toward Independence Pass to the east of Aspen with Black Sox, I understood that to follow His path, we must discard the old ways, learn new ones that are in keeping with God's word, and then implement them. We must become more like Christ every day in every way, in thought and through actions so we can be His true missionaries, his true ministers, to all seekers. And we must constantly stop and think about the wonderful blessings in our lives, the simple things, health, friends, family members, and freedom, all that I had forgotten during the days when fame had blinded me.

Without doubt, most people are looking for help, for someone to care enough about them to offer assistance. We never know what is going on in someone's life. He or she may look like they have it all, have it made, the nicest cars, the finest, most expensive homes, a wonderful family and yet even their closest friends or family may not be aware of their daily agonies dealing with addiction, depression, abuse, transgression, debt. No one is immune to trials and tribulations, and we all have the capacity to heal ourselves and others.

Perhaps I always knew these things, but my spiritual journey had truly awakened me, enlightened me to discard my toxic ways, and become a new person. After the choice to become a true minister in the lay sense of the word, I realized that I had to keep my eyes open and watch for others in distress. Sometimes it was just a "look" that told me they were seekers, or a few words they spoke. Time and time again, total strangers transfixed me with their sad stories, unloading problems that seemed insurmountable at the time. "No man is an island," as Thomas Dunne once wrote; everyone suffers at one time or another.

Certainly examples abounded in which the Good Lord brought people into my life that I could help. There was Sally, a brilliant Aspen woman whose legal problems and financial troubles were so great that she was living in her car; Janet, an African-American woman whom I met on a plane who told me about her mother's suffering from cancer; Cecelia, a beautiful young woman from New York City who had experienced sexual harassment at a major television network and was trying to get her life and reputation back; and Lois, married to a man she loved but whom she suspected of being obsessed with pornographic films, dating prostitutes, gambling, and excessive drinking. She didn't know whether to leave or stay with him because of their children. I gave Lois the mini-version of *The Purpose Driven Life* and suggested she pray, and pray, and pray some more, and then let God lead the way to her own salvation.

While contemplating the next step in my spiritual journey, Black Sox and I climbed in our trusty truck and headed for Santa Barbara, California. Besides its seaside charm, balmy ocean breezes, and the smell of fresh flowers, this city has always been a hotbed for writers. As I was exploring a Christian college just outside the city limits, the main purpose for the trip, I ran into more people seeking some sort of spiritual uplifting. One named Sara noticed Black Sox frolicking in the waves with three other dogs as I sat on the beach and watched him. Somehow I could tell she was in anguish, and so asked her if I could be of any help. She said that she was an aspiring actress with high hopes, but lived with a boyfriend whose condescension was hurting her. I listened to her story and told her prayer might help in learning what course of action God had in mind. I gave Sara a mini-copy of *The Purpose Driven Life* and told her I would help her any way I could. That night I prayed she could find spiritual relief to calm her troubled mind.

Helping Sara reminded me once again that many times our ministry, one possible without any formal education, may be to just sit quietly and listen. We all talk too much, and don't listen enough. Just opening one's heart to another can truly soothe a wounded soul.

As I continued listening to others, many confided in me, and I heard about how other men had experienced loneliness when divorce had ripped a good home life from their hands as it had mine. Steve loved his children more than anything, but he lost them to his drug abuse. Now he was on the road to recovery and I told him I would pray for him. Manny ran around with women, and when his wife discovered his clandestine affair, she left him. Through counseling, he was attempting to earn back her trust. I prayed for him as I did for a stepfather who missed his stepson as much as I missed my stepsons and stepdaughter. He and I talked about how Father's Day was something neither one of us had experienced in its truest form, and how disappointing that was to both of us.

One beacon of light was Pete, a man with considerable wealth who fell prey to the doom of drugs and alcohol. Pete reached rock bottom, found the Lord and began dedicating himself to helping others with similar problems. Through his participation in the *Purpose Driven Life* discussions, he decided to create a Bible study and gospel group on the weekends in Aspen. He was truly acting on God's will. Pete almost glowed with God's grace, and you could see him loving his new work of spreading God's Word and helping others. I encouraged him to seek the ministry by attending seminary, which he considered.

Billy, another of God's ministers, was small in stature, but big in heart. Billy had been through some rough times and was constantly questioning what God had in mind for him. In addition to his wonderful sense of humor, Billy was a skilled ventriloquist and juggler. After being a school bus driver for many years, he related well to children. When we spoke about God's purpose for him, I tried to be like Barnabas in the Bible and encouraged him to focus on youth ministry, spreading the Word of God as he dazzled youngsters with his God-given talents. I felt he could really make a great difference with many kids struggling with today's issues. Billy soon agreed that working with children and sharing God with them was his true calling.

As I related to Billy, when you are awake to the Spirit, to a higher power in action, you will see God's hand in everyday events. While leading the *Purpose Driven Life* discussion group, I witnessed amazing events that, just a few months earlier, I would have attributed to coincidence.

Many times, when the Holy Spirit acts, we may not understand why immediately. This is especially true, as I learned, when things don't go the way we want them to. After some time in Aspen, I figured this was where I was supposed to settle, and decided to invest in a reasonably priced (if there is such a thing in Aspen) condominium. After agreeing to the purchase, the inspection revealed structural damage to the foundation. Then I discovered a downtown location where I might open a small used bookstore, something Aspen sorely needed. But the landlord decided to wait so he could make more money combining that space with another. Lastly, the National Endowment for the Arts denied a grant for my literary foundation, Books for Life. Three disappointments in a row made me wonder just what the Good Lord was up to, and it would be a few weeks before I understood clearly how denying me was ultimately in my best interest.

In the midst of this confusion, on a warm Aspen morning, my New York literary agent called to ask whether I would accept a collaboration with the infamous former NBA great Dennis Rodman, one of the true legends of the game with five championship rings to his credit. Rodman played with the Detroit Pistons where he was a member of a group called the "bad boys," and with the Chicago Bulls, where he rebounded the ball for Michael Jordan. Rodman wanted to tell his story, one that had an inspirational twist to it. As an admitted scoundrel, woman chaser, and all-around self-centered jerk with trademark multi-colored hair and tattoos covering much of his upper torso, he was cleaning up his act in another attempt to play in the NBA. Curious to meet this controversial character, I traveled to Newport Beach, California where I joined Rodman and his agent for lunch at a seaside restaurant. I tried not to focus on the earrings sticking out of his ears and nose, and his rainbow-colored hair, but instead listened to his plans for the future. As the aroma of Dennis' fish tacos filled the air, I was impressed by how articulate he was. Dennis was obviously a bright man who had assumed his outrageous image to further his career. He seemed deeply interested in a new image and in preparing his body to compete with much younger, though less savvy, players.

When I returned to Aspen, I developed a proposal for a book entitled *The Worm Returns*, a play on words in reference to one of his nicknames, "The Worm." But New York publishers wanted little to do with Rodman until they knew for sure that he was rejoining the big leagues. When Rodman's return did not materialize, our book project was shelved. A short time later, a publishing company did offer us a deal, but rejected the book's inspirational undertone. I resisted the temptation to work with Rodman, and so another author took over writing the book with him, one that proved to be a disappointment.

Had I missed a chance to minister Rodman, who was clearly seeking some spiritual direction? Had the Holy Spirit sent me to him to assist with his redemption? Or was there another lesson I was being taught, that unless people are seriously devoted to changing their lives, change won't come easily? When I read about Rodman's legal troubles after we had met, I hoped that perhaps he might change for the better. Despite his flashy, crazed public persona, there was a good heart there, a caring heart that I had glimpsed during our lunch. I promised myself to pray for him in the hope that his life might find a new direction.

If there needed to be any further sign that my spiritual journey was continuing toward new growth, inspiration arrived when Rev. Rick Warren, author of *The Purpose Driven Life*, spoke at the Aspen Institute. I had just visited Saddleback Church, where he ministered, during my Southern California trip. Now I listened from a back row seat as Rev. Warren talked about each person's need, and duty, to discover the true purpose in his, or her, life. Clad in his classic Hawaiian shirt, he reiterated his best seller's outline. His message hit home, and when I spoke with him after the lecture about how the book had guided a transformation in my life and how I had led discussion groups in its honor, he smiled and told me to keep up the good work. As I left the speaking venue with an autographed book, I was determined to pay even more attention as to how, and where, the Spirit was leading me. To be certain, Rev. Warren's visit and our interaction forced me to consider what the Spirit was up to now, why this man whose book had helped turned my life around had appeared at this particular time.

One bright, beautiful Aspen morning when the sky was a deep blue like no other on the face of the Earth, as Black Sox and I walked along the Roaring Fork River toward a tributary where he loved to play with his tennis ball as the current made its way downstream, the idea suddenly hit me: "I want to go to seminary." There was no tap on the shoulder this time, no words like before when I was told to drive to Colorado, but the idea was there, put there I knew, by the Spirit that was constantly within me. No one knows why ideas like these strike us, why a light bulb turns on from inside our brains. During my writing adventures, nearly every title for a book came to me in the middle of the night. Apparently the Spirit was working overtime even when I was asleep.

Years earlier this notion of attending seminary would have seemed ludicrous. But this time, it did not. Whether I became an ordained minister or not, seminary, I intuitively knew, was the next logical step in my continuing spiritual journey. The gambler in me embraced risk when others might shy away. I had no idea if I could handle classroom study and tests again after having failed so miserably at academia most of my life. But the same mentality that made me love the poker game Texas Hold'em that I played in Aspen with such colorful characters as Jimmy Yeager, a local restaurateur, made me decide that giving seminary a shot made sense. Jimmy had added to my understanding of the Jewish faith when he honored me with an invite to a Seder, a Jewish feast marking the beginning of the Jewish holiday of Passover.

Heeding what others would later tag the "call," I began to scour the Internet and discovered Colorado Christian University (CCU) and the Iliff School of Theology in Denver. I decided to visit both.

As the snow melted on the mountains along my drive to Denver through Glenwood Springs and Vail during the early days of 2005, I felt a spiritual uplifting. Was this going to be a new chapter in my life, one that would permit me to know the Lord better than ever before? At sixty years old, was I about to embark on something very special, something the Good Lord surely had in mind for me?

Both CCU and Iliff intrigued me with their special programs, especially their degrees in Christian counseling, the area that interested me most. When an official at CCU informed me of the importance of strong academic references as part of the application requirements, I jokingly told him that might be tough since many of my professors were probably dead.

After the illuminating visits, I dropped into two Denver bookstores, the legendary Tattered Cover, and Barnes and Noble, where I perused the business section to research a few publishers for a friend of mine writing a business book. Suddenly, the book *Jesus, Life Coach*, by Laurie Beth Jones, literally jumped out of the shelf right into my hands. Scanning its pages, I knew this was a book the Good Lord wanted me to read.

When I returned to Aspen, I began to devour the book, and Jones' lesson about having Jesus as a "life coach." Each section seemed to speak to me directly regarding the life choices possible. One question immediately grabbed my interest: "What would you do if you only had six healthy months to live?" I was now over sixty, and although growing up I thought most people were dead by then, I lived by the tenet that, "You are only as old as you feel." And so I only truly felt twenty-five, if that, especially with Eddie as my pal. Kids have such enthusiasm, and he was no exception. One day when we had finished watching a Disney movie, he wanted to see it again, and again. He figured we could see it four times that day if we wanted to.

As I reread the question, "What would you do if you had six healthy months to live?" from a large boulder overlooking Black Sox scampering in the water below, I realized the answer for me was easy: to learn more about the Lord, the Bible, and Christian counseling. While I wanted to open a bookshop, continue the work of our literary foundation, perhaps write new books, and of course, become a husband and father, my priority was to become closer to God through further study of His message. I quickly returned to my writing studio where I filled out the application for the Iliff School of Theology, believing it to be the best choice for me. I even perused the University of Denver website to check on nearby housing possibilities.

While surfing the Internet, I searched for other possible Christian counseling seminary programs. The Spiritual Direction program at San Francisco Theological Seminary (SFTS) located in Marin County across the Golden Gate Bridge from San Francisco caught my eye. Interested in what it had to offer, I dialed the number only to discover the program was for those who were already ministers. But the woman told me that SFTS had some wonderful programs in theology. After inspecting the website, noting the beautiful nineteenth century buildings, I knew this was a seminary to consider. Without hesitation, I picked up the telephone and dialed the SFTS office again. When a cheerful woman named Catherine Oliver answered, I simply asked, "Do you let old people with bad grades in?"

―――――――――――――

When I mentioned the possibility to others that I might attend seminary, most, with the exception of my younger sister Debbie, thought I had finally lost my mind. But these same people had forgotten that curiosity was the one characteristic that had ruled my personality since early in life. I'm uncertain where this particular gene came from, but it had propelled me to keep digging, to keep learning, to keep pushing beyond the status quo, to keep traveling down a new road wherever it led. Alongside curiosity came the determination to try new things, to never worry about failure even though I failed many times. In turn, I had always heeded opportunities despite any lack of training, or knowledge, essentially "winging" it, and learning on the go by trial and error.

Now, as August 2005 approached, I was headed on another road trip into the unknown. One up-close look at the castle-like nineteenth century Scottish-stone buildings and the awe-inspiring mountaintop seminary in the spring had convinced me that San Francisco Theological Seminary was for me. This wasn't an easy decision, as Black Sox and I once again piled our belongings into the Chevy truck and a U-Haul trailer to hit the road, one leading from Aspen to San Francisco. I knew I would miss the small town, the many friends, and especially the wilderness area east of town where the Roaring Fork River guided hikers toward Independence Pass and Denver. There is no place on earth like Aspen with its mining history, famous visitors and residents, first-rate year-round cultural activities, and healing spirit emanating from the glorious beauty of the surrounding mountains. Saying good-bye to my little brother Eddie was tough, too. I never knew the exact reasons for his father's absence, but my leaving must have reminded Eddie of that loss. He had been a true blessing for me, a reminder of how much I loved children and still hoped to be a father one day.

Two days after leaving Aspen, with the seminary acceptance letter in hand and the enjoyment of the road trip along I-70 meandering through the majestic Rockies toward Salt Lake City, Reno and beyond, Black Sox and I pulled up to an apartment next to a walking trail on a mountaintop overlooking Sausalito harbor where he could romp around and enjoy the smells of coyotes, deer, and other wild animals. On that trail, we would meet many new dog lovers and friends, including Hugh and Pearl, and Debi, special pals to this day.

As we settled into our new apartment, and walked the adjacent trail where the view of the Sausalito harbor welcomed daily wonderment for the beauty of the area, I took stock of who Mark Shaw really was. I knew I had made strides in Aspen toward being the kind of Christian person I envisioned, but I knew I still had a long way to go. I was still immersed way too much in the real world instead of God's world, the spiritual world. I was also alone with no one to share my life with. On the outside, I probably appeared cheery and bright, but on the inside, there were days when I still felt confused.

Through the grace of the Good Lord and those in the admission office at SFTS, and a recommendation letter from my Aspen friend Dave Danforth, who argued in my SFTS application that my life as a suffering, ever-hopeful Chicago Cubs fan was evidence enough of my spiritual beliefs, I had received my notification of acceptance in July 2005. This sixty-year-old person, one who should have been considering retirement days at the beach, was about to embark on a scholastic adventure with a limited background in Christian education or church membership. Since the path was still unclear as to whether an MDiv (master of divinity) degree might be attainable or even warranted, the choice to enter the Master of Arts in Theological Studies program made sense. The core courses included biblical studies, church history, theology, ministry, and spirituality, with opportunities to enroll in electives from any of the sister Graduate Theological Union seminaries. There were nine seminaries in all, including the Pacific School of Religion (interdenominational), American Baptist Seminary, Franciscan School of Theology, and the Dominican School of Philosophy and Theology. One could also study specific areas of interest at the Center for Islamic Studies and the Asia Project.

The SFTS campus was perfect for a new seeker like me; I relished the half-hour chapel services four times a week, walking the grounds early in the morning with Black Sox when the quiet solitude permitted inner reflection, and talking with fellow students and faculty about their stories as to how God's entry into their lives had changed them forever.

The top-notch classroom instruction introduced me to new ways of thinking. Travels through the Torah (the first five books of the Bible), Acts, and the Gospels satiated my thirst for insight. Suddenly faced with writing academic papers, the Holy Spirit guided me along as I penned "The Mind of Luke Revisited," and "The Parable of the Wicked Tenants: A Matter of Perspective."

I was enlightened through the process of writing an explanatory paper about the connection between Paul's concept of sin and the novel *The Plague* by Albert Camus. Understanding how the plague— sin disguised as disease—infiltrated the citizenry of Camus' city of Oran provided the perfect springboard for learning why Paul believed that sin occurred in all of those who do not follow God's Word. Two thousand years have made little difference between the early Christians and those of today who continue to chase false gods in hope of discovering happiness and contentment. One false god is certainly fame. I learned that.

A particular systematic theology course forced me to ponder questions such as: Is there a God? If so, who is S/He and how did S/He create the world? If so, why does S/He permit suffering in the world? Along the way, I was introduced to various theories on these subjects and others through the writings of such expert theologians as H. Richard Niebuhr, Paul Tillich, Karl Barth, Martin Luther and John Calvin. My education was illuminating, and I soaked up every word from the many lectures and books made available to me.

I never missed a class during my days at seminary, grateful as I was for this opportunity to learn. Better still, I achieved a goal that was paramount in my mind of never making a fool of myself. Since I had a modest background in theological study, and most of my classmates had been immersed in such study since birth, I monitored what I said in class so that no one would learn of my very limited knowledge. Several times I held my breath as I asked, or answered, a question hoping that no one would turn toward me with a "man, what an idiot" glare. I kidded Doug Olds, one student who impressed me with his biblical intellect, that I was going to have him banned from class because he was simply "too smart." But Doug and the others helped me through, helped me achieve my goal of not embarrassing myself.

Leo Tolstoy's brilliant short novel *The Death of Ivan Ilych*, illustrating Ilych's pursuit of self-centered goals, money, lofty position, and notoriety, illuminated my greater understanding of Niebuhr's views on "little-g gods," and the connection between literature and theology, between one's creative and personal life. One only has to recall that Dante in his classic, *The Divine Comedy*, referred to self-centered souls as condemned to Hell because they lacked human charity for one another. I was accepting my own sins of worshipping false idols such as money, power, and also fame, as diseased addictions.

While courses in biblical studies, history, theology and ethics were insightful, it was the areas of ministry and spirituality that produced the greatest inner change in me as I continued my path toward a true Oneness with God. While *The Purpose Driven Life* had changed my life for the better, and *Jesus, Life Coach* had propelled me toward seminary, the books discovered through a class called Spiritual Life and Leadership shaped who I was to become. *Listening for the Soul* by Jean Stairs expresses the author's ideas about pastoral counseling's transformative nature when we truly put ourselves into the spirit-space of another person. If the book *Listening for the Soul* was my introduction to contemplative listening, it was also my entrée to the works of Thomas Merton, the famous Catholic monk and mid-twentieth-century spiritual writer, and author of nearly seventy books including *The Seven Storey Mountain, No Man Is an Island, Wisdom of the Desert,* and *Zen and the Birds of Appetite.* Merton was a spiritual man of inclusion, not exclusion, one who believed that all religions and spiritualities had more in common than not. Critics have applauded Merton's views on any number of subjects. Dutch priest and spiritualist Henri Nouwen called Merton "the most important spiritual writer of the twentieth century." Noted author Anne Lamott (*Traveling Mercies, Bird by Bird*) has acknowledged that, "a [great deal] of my spiritual seeking began with Thomas Merton. He [was] an incredible source of light and comfort and humor." When Merton unexpectedly died in 1968, His Holiness the Dalai Lama told reporters, "I felt that I had lost personally one of my best friends, and one who was a contributor for harmony between different religions and for mental peace."

Just a week or two into seminary, I was assigned one of Merton's most famous books, *New Seeds of Contemplation,* as an examination into "the contemplative life." From the first day I read the famous monk's words, the concepts of living a contemplative life riveted me, and I wondered how I might lead one. Merton guided my thoughts and corralled my feelings toward a better understanding of my true self and purpose.

What resonated more than anything for me was Merton's prolific directives about shedding the mask we all use to hide our "false self" from others. I had tried too hard to be the person I thought I was supposed to be based on so many outside influences. Merton wrote in *New Seeds of Contemplation,* "We are at liberty to be real, or to be unreal. We may be true or false, the choice is ours. We may wear now one mask and now another, and never, if we so desire, appear with our own true face . . . causes have effects, and if we lie to ourselves, and to others, then we cannot expect to find truth and reality whenever we happen to want them. If we have chosen the way of falsity we must not be surprised that truth eludes us when we finally come to need it!" Merton also explained, "Every moment and every event of every man's life on earth plants something in his soul." This made perfect sense since my adventures had certainly planted many seeds in mine.

I later realized that Merton was talking about himself; his wisdom stemmed from his own experiences. He also wrote in *New Seeds of Contemplation*, "This is the man that I want to be but who cannot exist, because God does not know anything about him," Merton was right; God did not know me because I had worn a mask for so many years. Merton's words on the subject of writing certainly hit home. He wrote:

> If you write for God, you will reach many men and bring them joy. If you write for men—you make some money and you may give someone a little joy and you make a noise in the world, for a little while. If you write for yourself, you can read what you have written and after ten minutes you will be so disgusted you will wish you were dead.

During a break in my studies, Merton's wisdom highly influenced me completing *Dandelions In The Moonlight*, a novel inspired by the life of a German Christian woman imprisoned in the camps during the Holocaust. Forced to trust a dreaded Nazi prison guard when an orphaned Russian girl she is hiding faces danger, the lead character Vera (named after my mother) learns how love may replace hate when God intervenes and soothes the heart and soul. Writing about the little girl made me ponder the perils youngsters face and how adults must protect them at all costs.

Meanwhile, Merton's inspiring words continued to impact my soul when I learned more about his conversion process. There was a more human side to Merton than most people knew about, and his struggles with pre-monastic sinful conduct, including alcoholism and adultery, made me realize that even—or perhaps especially— saint-like people have dark sides, too. Merton has traveled with me as a spiritual companion ever since.

From the outset, Dr. Lewis Rambo, in his course Pastoral Care and Counseling, emphasized the need to serve those experiencing turmoil and to do so with compassion and love. A pastor, or for that matter, anyone ministering, should always be in the process of self-care, and spiritual, psychological, and intellectual growth.

While the learning process continued, I adopted the mantra: "Teach me, lead me, guide me, oh Lord, I pray." Repeating these words often kept me on my spiritual road, one where I was constantly listening for the voice of God. During walks with Black Sox around the seminary paths where vibrant flowers greeted us at every turn, I would sing softly, "How blessed I am, How blessed I am, How blessed I am, Oh Lord" to remind myself of the continuing blessings I was receiving.

As always during the spiritual journey, I prayed for my stepchildren and my ex-wife. Word reached me that she had remarried. I was pleased for her, pleased that she had found someone to share her life. During the summer months of 2004 and 2005, I thought I might hear from at least one of the boys or Kimberly as Father's Day approached, but I never did. Though I was hurt by the slight, I tried hard to let it go and move on, and held on to Rev. Warren's teaching that those who hurt us usually forget what they have done, while we carry the burden around with us. We experience pain, he said, while they don't care anymore, having moved on with their lives. In essence, they are free while we are still bound by the bad experience, the disappointment, the hurt. I was determined to shed the shackles that bound me, to truly be free, to focus on the good times I had experienced with my stepchildren, and forget the messy days since the separation and divorce. This was a daily challenge, but I knew I was making progress.

New friends made the task easier. Several Korean seminary students needed help with their writing skills, and adjustment to American life. I edited several papers, and even taught one woman how to drive. Across from my apartment near the seminary lived Dae Seop, a gentle and calm man. His writing reflected a blend of Eastern and Western theology and I learned much from him about how spirituality had led him toward the ministry. Dae Seop had two small children and I enjoyed watching him play with them. He never raised his voice, and the children respected his authority.

The Study of Religion and Cinema, and Art and Religion, two courses offered at the Graduate Theological Union by a gifted professor, Dr. Doug Adams, opened my eyes to the presence of religion in all aspects of life. A new course by Dr. Rambo heightened my interest on the religious conversion process. I fulfilled the class' term paper requirement by focusing on the conversion of Thomas Merton, a complicated man who had struggled with his religiousity since childhood.

When I learned of Merton's late-life love affair with a student nurse half his age, I couldn't help but ask, *Why?* The more I researched, the more I was intrigued by how the romance affected his conversion process. My paper entitled "Sponge Baths, Sensuous Kisses, and Secret Rendezvous: The Rollercoaster Conversion Ride of Thomas

Merton" was only an initiation into my continued investigation into and affiliation for Merton's fascinating life.

Those who decide to become ministers are in truth ministers as soon as they step through the seminary door. Immersing oneself in its spiritual environment—in the buildings, the chapel, and the library, and with the students, the educators, and the course curriculum—transforms those seeking enlightenment into God's messengers. Those who attend seminary are never the same again. The Holy Spirit grabs hold of one's heart and soul. When God takes over, the old person truly dies, or at least nears death, and a new person is created. The new person abandons any sense of false self and becomes free from the rigors of the real world. The seminary life, like the monastic life, may, if the person permits it, if the person seeks it, convert the person to the true Christian he or she hopes to be. This new person, this new child of God, now filled with love and compassion, relinquishes control to make way for the timeless presence of the Holy Spirit. As Thomas Merton explains, one has to die to live, has to empty to be full, and has to shed any sense of life adverse to the will of God so as to do the will of God.

What I was learning was to take notice each day if my train was still on the metamorphosis track, not wavering or backsliding into my old self. Nearing the end of the transformation, it felt as if my new self was standing on the sidelines and watching his life go by. I was viewing my life in the context of God's perspective and reason, allowing God's will to take over my brain to ensure that my actions never stem from anger, frustration, disappointment, fear, vindictiveness, jealousy, or any other non-Christlike emotion, but rather from love and compassion. Any ill feeling I had toward my stepchildren was diminishing; I understood they still loved me, but that our separation was inevitable. I had forgiven them, as I hoped they had forgiven me, and I was in the process of forgiving myself for my irreverent behavior. While I had made mistakes, mistakes were part of human failing, part of my weakness in desiring to be a big shot, to be famous. I was ready to move on, and looking back, I understood that somebody had to stand up to Bobby Knight, and I was that somebody, pushed into the fray by a higher power determined to teach life lessons to us both. I had been guilty of causing my family pain even if my intentions were quite the opposite. Instead of beating myself up about it, however, I suddenly felt a calm, a feeling of inner peace, similar to what had overcome me in Aspen.

With this blessed mindset, I began working with a group of intercity kids in Marin City, just north of Sausalito. Underprivileged children there needed assistance with the rigors of homework. Each week we met in a church where two African-American youngsters, about the same age as the triplets when I first met them, sat on either side of me. Like most kids that age, homework was the last thing on their minds, but I was patient with them as I had been with my stepchildren years earlier. One boy, Alexander, was very bright but lacked any writing skills. I knew the Good Lord had brought him to me. Being with Alexander, and watching the other kids with their mentors reinstated so many memories. The church was abuzz with learning, and the kids were there because their parents loved them enough to bring them each week.

Without doubt, true blessings were flowing my way. If this was not enough, the Good Lord had a partner in mind for me—a woman to love, and to be loved by, a mystical, gentle woman, a soul mate, one with whom I could share an endless spiritual journey.

BOOK IV

CHAPTER NINE

Gentle Flower Petal

During the first months of seminary, when the owner decided to move close to Vancouver, I assumed the lease of a small bookshop called Cricket's in downtown Sausalito on Princess Street, just one block from the bay. As sea gulls danced on the water, and ships appeared daily on the horizon headed under the Golden Gate Bridge toward the Far East, tourists from all parts of the world flocked to the multitude of stores along Bridgeway, the street closest to the water. Soon I had special friends like photographer Koren Reyes; Debbie Dewey, a transplanted Texan who helped in the shop; Charlie from the leather store; Bob and Rosemary, two gifted artists; Peter and Lily, owners of a flower shop; and Bill Smith, my upstairs neighbor."

I loved books, and hoped that the income from Cricket's, with Black Sox as the store mascot, would help pay for my theological studies. Never one to be much of a businessman, I couldn't sustain a positive cash flow, but meeting the multi-cultured tourists who stopped by was worth the effort. My friend Hugh Campion, a former TWA pilot turned stage actor extraordinaire, helped out when I was at seminary classes. One day, he told me he hadn't charged sales tax because "he didn't feel like it." We laughed about that comment for months to come. Hugh also enjoyed the time a customer asked me the price of a book and I said, "Oh, either two or three dollars." No wonder the store was a financial flop.

While Cricket's stocked worthy used books including some classic children's volumes (the Nancy Drew series, Dr. Seuss' works), my aim was to mix in as many spiritual books as possible including *The Purpose Driven Life, New Seeds of Contemplation,* and ones delineating the Eastern religions. I also had some copies of the Qur'an, a bestseller on atheism, and several specifically about Buddhism. For a time, the store hosted a group of people who discussed *The Purpose Driven Life.* Many were nonbelievers, or highly critical of the book, which allowed for some lively discussions and practice with the education I was exposed to at seminary.

Among the new books we stocked was *Melvin Belli, King of the Courtroom,* my eighteenth published book. Belli, the legendary San Francisco attorney, had represented the Rolling Stones, Mohammed Ali, and Jack Ruby, among many other (in)famous clients. I had completed the book before attending seminary, but just before the release date, the publisher, who had known Belli personally, died, resulting in a less than enthusiastic promotion campaign. The same kind of unfortunate timing impaired my book about spy Jonathan Pollard released within days after 9/11. Nobody wanted to talk about spies, and that book, while critically acclaimed, fell far short of sales expectations.

On Sundays, I semi-regularly attended the Sausalito Presbyterian Church up the hill from Cricket's where Jim Burklo was minister. This was a very progressive church, but it was not what I was looking for. Instead, Black Sox and I traveled the half hour north toward

Stinson Beach where we could roam and he could play in the surf and dig, and dig, and dig in the sand. How I enjoyed the peace and tranquility of watching him play as seagulls paraded before me, as the surf bounced and pounded against the earthen soil. Most days, there was no one around except for us, and Black Sox and I cherished the quiet, the wonderful world of the quiet. Seminary classes and activities and days working at the store took up most of my time, but the hours Black Sox and I spent at the beaches or roaming the mountain trails around the area were truly a time I spent alone with God as a true contemplative. Here I felt I was one with the Spirit; here I felt the inner, joyful peace; here I could pray and thank the Good Lord for my blessings.

While living in Aspen, I had visited my brother Jack and his wife Sue at their home in Coldwater, Michigan. They raised and showed Clydesdales. After falling in love with the gentle giants, I asked whether there had been a history written of the legendary animals with the furry white "feathers" covering their ankles.

One thing led to another, and I was commissioned to write a book about the Clydesdales from their earliest origins in Scotland to present day. Black Sox had to stay behind, but I flew to London, promptly got lost, and then drove to the lush fields of Scotland where I soon stood next to the roaring water of the Falls of Clyde. The surrounding countryside was breathtaking with horses milling through the thick green grass, but the thrill of the trip was spending time with John Zawadzki and his wife, who bred Clydesdales. Standing next to one of their horses made me look like a shrimp. These huge animals were truly a miracle of God's making, and their gentleness something to behold.

Using the research material and the photographs I collected, I wrote a coffee-table book entitled *Clydesdales: The World's Most*

Magical Horse. The release of the book was set for the Wisconsin State Fair in Milwaukee, but printing problems caused a fateful delay.

By early October, during my first seminary semester, the book arrived. At the request of the draft horse association, I headed for the annual draft horse show in the Michigan State University (MSU) Pavilion in East Lansing, Michigan. After signing books for a couple of hours, I walked down to the show ring where several Clydesdale teams were competing. Standing by the railing was a beautiful Asian woman with flowing black hair and dancing brown eyes. After she offered to move over to let my sister Debbie stand next to me by the rail, I began talking to her with interest. My marriage breakup was behind me, and the effects of the Knightmare had worn off. I was ready to love again.

During a brief conversation, I learned that the woman's name was Wen-ying Lu. She was originally from Taiwan and now worked as a cataloger and linguistics librarian at MSU. At first I thought she was married since she wore a wedding ring. I asked if her husband was somewhere in the pavilion. Mistakenly presuming the woman next to me was my wife (not my sister), Lu felt safe to tell me her husband, Juergen, was there in spirit. He had died a few years before.

Immediately, I knew I wanted to know more about this lovely woman as I had for some time believed that I was going to meet someone special soon. Thinking quickly, I told her I wanted to gift a copy of the Clydesdale book to her library, but I would have to know where to send it. Lu gave me her business card. Before we parted, I introduced her to my sister Debbie and my brother Jack and his wife Sue standing nearby. The moment I landed back in Sausalito, I e-mailed Lu that the book was on the way. I also asked whether she would like to visit the Bay Area at my expense with no strings attached. When she said "yes" with the conditions that she pay her own expenses, and stay with a friend, my heart jumped fifty beats.

Before Lu's visit, we talked on the telephone, and I learned more about her. She went by her last name Lu, which was easier for Americans to pronounce and remember. She had been born in Taipei, Taiwan, but grew up in Kaohsiung, a city by the sea in the southwestern part of the country. She had three younger sisters, ones she referred to as Number 2, 3, and 4, nicknames her father gave the girls to encourage them to practice English. Her mother had died years earlier, and her father was living with two of her sisters.

Two years after graduating from college, Lu decided to pursue an advanced degree in linguistics so that she could be qualified to teach college. In 1985, she began her studies at the University of Illinois at Urbana-Champaign (UIUC). As she discovered the lack of teaching positions back in Taiwan when she defended her dissertation, she decided to apply for and was admitted to the Graduate School of Library and Information Science at UIUC. Upon graduation, she had accepted a job at Michigan State University Libraries as a librarian. It was quite interesting to consider that an author like me who loved books had found a librarian who also loved books.

During her visit, one featuring our seaside dinner in Sausalito with her friends Suchuin and Ron as chaperones, and a visit with her cousin Chi-ju, there was love in the air, but we had to overcome one obstacle immediately. Lu was afraid of dogs. She had been bitten when she was a child, and so I held my breath when she first met Black Sox to see how she might react. To my relief, the two of them became fast friends as he swayed her in his loving way. Black Sox was the perfect role model since he loved everyone, strangers included;

he was always composed, never held a grudge when left alone (a rarity), and was at ease whether it was raining or sunny. He also didn't care if it was day or night or what day, month, or year it was. Give him his rubber balls, a blanket to hide them in, a rawhide bone once in a while, two square meals per day, two or three walks, a tummy rub or three, and numerous rides in the truck with the back window down so he could poke his head out, and he was happy.

Now that Lu had fallen for Black Sox as I had when he was a puppy, our love affair was full speed ahead despite the long distance. Months later, Lu's father was diagnosed with stomach cancer and she traveled to Taiwan for his surgery. After she returned, I proposed and to my delight, Lu accepted. When we informed my family members at a dinner, my sister Anne said to Lu, "You've made a good choice. Mark is low maintenance."

When Lu's father's condition worsened, she traveled to Taiwan again. She was at his bedside when he passed away. After she returned to Michigan, I shared the grief with her.

According to Taiwanese customs, one could get married within one hundred days of a parent's passing and have a very small and modest wedding, or one had to wait for three years. Lu and I discussed our options and decided we wanted to get married soon.

When I told my friend Debbie and her husband Ken of our intention, they offered their small ship for our nuptials. The ceremony was performed by a ship's captain on July 4, 2006 in San Francisco Bay near Angel Island and the Golden Gate Bridge. As the sun shone brightly, and the wind rustled our hair, Black Sox, wearing a Salvador Dali tie for the event given to him by Dave Danforth, my sister Debbie, her husband David, and several close friends joined us for the blessed ceremony. Lu looked so beautiful, and photographs later captured my exuberance as we stood on the ship's bow and held each other close.

Not only did I find the new love of my life, a true companion, and a brilliant woman who had earned her PhD, but one who was a shining light in so many ways. Her first name meant "gentle flower petal," certainly appropriate for a woman so lovely. This love with Lu was different from the one I enjoyed with Chris, but both were special. Some people who knew me best believed that I had married Chris more because of my love for the stepchildren and their need for a stepfather who had the time to be with them, than for Chris. But I did not believe this was true. I genuinely cared for her, and would always recall the wonderful times we had spent together. Perhaps in the future, I hoped, there could be some sort of reconciliation, a time when she and I, and Kimberly, Kyle, Kevin, and Kent, could gather, leave the past in the past, and start anew.

When Lu and I enjoyed a belated honeymoon in Paris, what I had learned about religious art came in handy when we visited magical venues such as the Abbey Church of Saint Denis, the Louvre, the Sainte-Chapelle, Notre Dame de Paris, and the Rodin Museum where August Rodin's *The Thinker* mesmerized us. We also enjoyed a fascinating exhibit of Robert Rauschenberg's at the Centre Pompidou, Paris' chic modern-art museum. The exhibition included his famous work, *Monogram*, a creation featuring a goat—an angora, stuffed, horned goat to be more specific—with a black tire wrapped around its midsection.

A major point of concern when Lu and I first met was our respective spiritualities. Lu accepted my being a Christian but wanted to know if I was one of those far-right fundamentalists with extreme views. I assured her I was not. She was raised in the Confucian/

Buddhist/Taoist world but was not absolute in any one belief. Would our two worlds of spirituality conflict and divide us or was there common ground where a loving relationship could blossom? After many discussions, we realized that our ideologies shared many more commonalities than differences and we began to meld into a loving couple with an exhilirating spiritual oneness. During a most memorable discussion when I talked about my following the teachings of Jesus, she blurted out, "Well, he sounds like a good role model." I had never thought about it that way but she was right. Even if someone did not believe in Jesus' existence, his teachings could be guideposts to live by.

To learn more about Lu's culture and her upbringing, we traveled to Taiwan where I met her sisters and other relatives. I attended Lu's uncle's funeral with her and followed the Chinese/Taiwanese tradition of bowing and kowtowing several times to pay respect to this uncle as a nephew-in-law was supposed to do. Lu and her family had not asked me to follow the tradition due to my Christian faith, but greatly appreciated my adaptability when I did.

We had a grand time all around, especially riding on the high-speed train traveling from one end of the island to the other. Lu later joked that "Mark almost starved to death" to friends because of my dislike of Taiwanese food. She was right. I was a spoiled American who thought all Taiwanese food unattractive, gray and slimy. Thank goodness we found a Taiwanese-Italian restaurant or I would have only survived on a diet of rice and soy sauce.

While there, we decided my ailing feet might be soothed through a foot massage. Lu and her sister Number 4 escorted me to a middle-aged fellow in a massage parlor. For thirty minutes, I experienced agonizing pain as this cheerful man dug into my feet with fingers as strong as steel. The pain kept increasing in intensity and I thought my toes might fall off. I was in tears, and so was the Taiwanese fellow next to me. He was a regular client in fact. All the while, Lu and Number 4 sat across from us laughing and having the best time while I was in agony. They kept saying, "No pain, no gain." Finally, the ordeal ended, and while my feet felt much better, I swore there would never be any more Taiwanese foot massages for me during this lifetime.

Lu's contribution to my spiritual growth added layers to the Christlike person I was becoming. The journey, the next step in the perpetual road trip that marked the seasons of my life, had begun when God hit me over the head and told me I had to change my ways through the pain of the Knightmare. The study Bible and *The Purpose Driven Life* had laid the foundation for what I needed to learn by giving me a path to follow. Then, the teaching of *The Purpose Driven Life* class in Aspen added substance to what I was learning. My classes and experiences at SFTS brought another dimension to my learning. Now, Lu was with me, sharing ideas and thoughts both through our loving relationship and through her observations about the Christlike existence. I believe God brought her along for many reasons, but one was to make me question my beliefs and decide if I was truly going to be God's child or continue as the egotistical person I had been in the past. Was I truly a new person or just hiding my true self behind a mask? Had the scales blinding my eyes been removed like those of Paul on the road to Damascus? Such thoughts led me to Psalm 40 where I asked myself whether I was the person who had been saved according to the writings: "I waited patiently for the Lord; He turned to me and heard me cry. He lifted me out of the slimy pit, out of the mud and mire; He set my feet on a rock, and gave me a firm place to stand."

Certainly the Lord had lifted me into a love affair without equal. As the days and then months passed, Lu showed me what true, unconditional love entailed. She had the kindest, most loving heart and wanted to help others however possible. During my journey, I prayed for such an automatic and loving nature. Watching her in action was enlightening. She was my role model as I tried to emulate her actions, ones straight from a soul that was full of love and compassion. God had sent me a partner, exactly the right one, at exactly the right time.

Lu was able to share with me an experience in New York City we would both never forget. In honor of the fiftieth anniversary of Don Larsen's World Series perfect game, we were invited to attend a gala celebration. Upon entering the grand ballroom, we were amazed to learn that Don and his wife Corrine had allotted us seats at their table. When the dinner and program began, there we were seated between the Larsens and Yogi Berra, one of the great folk heroes of baseball, and his wife. To celebrate Don's achievement, many of those who had pitched perfect games stopped by to say hello to Don and Yogi and we met many of them. Being part of the history of the game reminded me of a previous trip to New York when Don had arranged for me to visit Yankee Stadium with the aid of a media pass. Sitting in the Yankee dugout, I felt the aura of players such as Babe Ruth, Lou Gehrig, Joe DiMaggio, and Mickey Mantle who had sat right where I was. I also was able to listen to manager Joe Torre talk about the current Yankee team. Not a bad seat for a good fielding, no-hit shortstop Little League player from Auburn, Indiana.

During the final half of my seminary experience, Lu assisted me with my readings on any number of subjects, and with my papers, especially formatting footnotes. But she also helped me in so many intangible ways. I was no longer alone; Black Sox and I had a woman who loved us both. I had come full circle from the days when my marriage had broken into a million pieces; I was free to love and be loved.

During the first year and a half of our marriage, Lu and I traveled back and forth from Michigan, where she continued her MSU library duties, to California while I completed seminary. We crossed the United States three times in our truck with Black Sox in the back seat. First, we traveled the middle route through California, Nevada, Colorado, Kansas, and on to Michigan; then we took the northern route back through Wisconsin, Minnesota, South Dakota, Utah, Wyoming, and Nevada. During our final trip, we traveled the southern route through California, lower Nevada, Arizona, New Mexico, Texas, Oklahoma, Missouri and Illinois. Through our adventure out West, we visited Aspen, Mount Rushmore, the Grand Canyon, Sedona, Taos, Jackson Hole, and Santa Fe. Black Sox got to play in the Roaring Fork River, the Snake River, and many rivers in between. It was a marvelous time to be certain, one when Lu and I learned more about each other's heritage and childhood experiences. We also talked about having a child, but both of us were concerned about advanced age. I was over sixty, and Lu over forty-five, which meant that any pregnancy would be high risk.

Was it really fair, we also wondered, to bring a child into the world who might lose one of his or her parents before he/she was a teenager? These thoughts consumed many discussions and we decided that having a child did not make the best sense. I could accept our decision, one made in the best interest of Lu and the child. Certainly there would be no Father's Days ahead, but this was okay. The Lord had blessed me with the perfect mate. I could not ask for anything more.

When I completed seminary with a master's degree in theological studies in two and a half years, was I a new person? Certainly I gleaned satisfaction from excelling at SFTS with a near straight A average (it's amazing what one may accomplish when one actually studies). I was proud of the achievement, although I was not yet completely transformed into a Christian, Christlike man who never exhibited the old Mark Shaw emotions towards others. The road to Christian perfection is never ending, filled with potholes at every turn. Regardless, the seminary experience had added its layer, its important layer, to the new, ever-evolving Mark Shaw. Instead of the "me" person, the angry person whom Bob Knight and others had tolerated just a few short years before, I now realized it wasn't about me. I had become a true disciple of the Holy Spirit, revolutionized, transformed, and converted into a different human being, a loving, forgiving, and calmer man, albeit still searching for the right way as new challenges appeared. And when they did, I would be standing on a true spiritual foundation to guide me. At some point, a friend asked me what "spiritual" meant, and I replied that, according to my definition, religion asks questions, and spirituality questions answers. A curious person, I considered myself a spiritual being, one who was always probing, always wanting to learn more. This explanation helped when people asked what had happened to my entertainment career, why I was no longer on television, why I was a "media dropout." I told them that part of my life was over, I had done that, been in the spotlight, been famous. Now I wanted to push ahead, not look back. With Lu by my side, and a new attitude to guide me, I welcomed each day with a fresh look at life's blessings.

In nineteenth-century author James Allen's book, *As a Man Thinketh*, whose title derives from Proverbs 23:7: "As a man thinketh in his heart, so is he," I read that, "Each of us is literally what we think, our character being the complete sum of all our thoughts." Allen later added, "We are what we think we are. If our mind has evil thoughts, we will suffer pain; if our thoughts are pure, joy will follow." Such words reminded me of my previous evil thoughts, the ego-driven ones that caused so much pain after the Knightmare. Those thoughts were now gone, expired, dead forever. In their place, "pure" thoughts, good ones, had certainly brought joy into my life in many ways, not the least of which was Lu. One day when I considered how blessed I was, I decided that every week I would give her a card with loving words written on it, reminding me of how special it was having her by my side. Sometimes I hid the card in the freezer, beside her pillow, or in the bathroom sink. I never forgot anniversaries or holidays. One year, I bought her a lawn mower, another year a tall ladder, a handy shovel, and a dandelion digger, yet another a towel warmer, a crochet bag, and a box of Alaskan sockeye salmon. These gifts don't sound too romantic, but I believe it was the caring thoughts behind them that made the difference.

As time passed, Lu and I adjusted to each other, giving new meaning to the term "opposites attract." She is frugal (her favorite words are "on sale" and "garage sale"); I am not. She is cautious; I am spontaneous. She is detailed; I am not. She doesn't get Woody Allen's sense of humor; I can't quit laughing. One product of her Chinese culture is, for example, to say, "Would you like to go to the farmer's market?" when she has already decided she wants to go, but won't say so. In other words, she is an expert of indirect communication. Many times I have to concentrate on what she is saying so I understand what she really means. I try to give her a straight answer;

she will often say, "It depends." If you ask Lu whether the sun will rise in the morning, she will take a few seconds, and then reply, "It could." We joke that she would drive courtroom lawyers and judges crazy because she rarely will answer with a "yes" or "no." Regardless, we hold the same values and ethics and have discovered a mutual respect and love for each other. One thing is for certain—I would never have made it through seminary without her.

At the graduation ceremony in California, I was the old guy wearing a cap and gown. Friends celebrated with me, Lu, and Black Sox. So many times in life I had fallen short of a goal. This time I accomplished what I intended. At times, I deliberated returning to seminary to earn a master of divinity degree so as to become ordained, but deep inside I knew this was not what the Spirit had in mind for me.

After moving to Michigan full time, I enjoyed living in East Lansing as I began to meet new friends and enjoy the college-town atmosphere. Neighbors Sandra (a gifted playwright) and James Seaton (MSU professor and author) provided great conversations about many topics. Book blogger Bill Castanier became a good friend, and Lu's MSU colleagues made me feel right at home upon my return to the Midwest. Lu and I also befriended Yin Pan, a Chinese accounting student through the MSU Friendship Family Program. Among Lu's MSU colleagues and friends, I found Ranti Junus' boyfriend Gene Dillenburg to commiserate with me over our beloved Chicago Cubs, and Kate Ojibway to care for Black Sox like he was her own dog.

We also enjoyed hosting an International Thomas Merton Society discussion group in our home. Most times I was overwhelmed with the biblical knowledge many possessed, including Dr.

Rudy Bernard, an MSU professor emeritus who had known Merton while briefly considering monkdom at the Abbey of Gethsemani in Kentucky where Merton also resided.

Lu is a woman with a tenacious spirit who succeeded in earning her doctorate by depositing her dissertation *ten years* after its successful defense. The university provided her with substantial challenges at the library among supportive colleagues she most respected.

I treasured my new friendship with Bob Baldori, or "Boogie Bob," as he was called. The founder of the rock band The Woolies (known for their hit record including the song *Who do you Love?* with Bo Diddley), Bob had also played piano with the legendary Chuck Berry. But his passion was boogie-woogie, and nobody played it better than Boogie Bob, especially when he teamed up with another legend, Bob Seeley. Together they toured the country and beyond, as far as Russia. When Lu and I heard them play their twin pianos, it was like Mozart had appeared in duplicate to try his hand at a new type of upbeat.

Across our street, the Kortemeyers, Anna and Gerd, had two wonderful kids, Daniel, and Christine. Neither had reached the age of ten yet, and I so enjoyed watching them as they played in their yard. At times, they would visit our home to play with Black Sox or to shoot some hoops with me on our driveway. On one special occasion at their home, they sat beside me at the dining room table. A photograph capturing the moment showed them laughing as Daniel put two fingers above my head like rabbit ears. Hearing them laugh made me and Lu laugh. With all of these blessings, perhaps Mark Shaw had finally found a home where he could live out his remaining days, ending his nomadic lifestyle once and for all.

Lu and I traveled together during the summer of 2007 to the Abbey of Gethsemani near Louisville, Kentucky where Thomas

Merton studied and wrote. Nearby, we enjoyed a spiritual retreat sponsored by the Merton Institute for Contemplative Living. Our leader, gifted scholar and author Jonathan Montaldo, led us through many of Merton's thoughts and ideas as we explored the path of contemplative living. I decided to write a new, fresh biography of Merton, one patterned after the SFTS paper I had written about his conversion process.

This book, like all of my others, was born of a question: Why did this famous monk fall madly in love with Margie Smith, a student nurse half his age, risking banishment from the monastic order and scandal for him and the Catholic Church? This was followed by another question: If this monk was the true, converted Christian he appeared to be from his writings, then why was he tempted in the first place?

Learning about Merton and his quest to become a free man would be an exciting experience for me, and one guided by the Holy Spirit every step of the way. Each day as I researched and wrote for the book, the Spirit took over and carried me to new revelations explaining why Merton found his true love at age fifty-one. Like me with Lu, he had discovered a connection to a partner who had taught him what loving, and being loved, was all about.

If there was one ultimate lesson to be learned from Merton, it dealt with the concept of uncertainty. Through my research and his writings, I was convinced that Merton faced uncertainty throughout his pre-Margie years. Like me, he was a restless soul, one who was continually searching, seeking some sort of tranquility and peace in his life but never finding it. He was supposed to be a converted Christian, supposed to be a dedicated monk who loved his God, supposed to be the peaceful, contented monk promoted by the

Catholic Church through his publications. This public persona triggered uncertainty in Merton as he was one thing to his followers and the general public, and another in his own private world. Only when he learned about true love in the form of Margie could he finally say he was certain about who he was, certain that he loved God more than anything, including the woman he had searched for his whole life. Merton's story was inspirational in nature—the story of a man who overcame agony and depression to find the Light and, consequentially, personal freedom.

To further research Merton's early life when he lived in Europe, Lu and I visited Venice, Florence, and the mystical village of Assisi where we felt the spirit of St. Francis from beginning to end. We then spent several days in Rome. Besides enjoying the historical aspects of this fabled city, we chose to visit Rome for the *pensione* where Thomas Merton stayed when he was eighteen, and where he experienced his father's ghost, a true defining moment in his life. One morning, as if the Holy Spirit were guiding us along, we found the Piazza Barberini at the intersection of Via Sistina and Via Tritone. There, amidst other landmarks such as the Triton Fountain, the Bristol Hotel, the Barberini Cinema, and the Barberini Palace, we spotted the *pensione*. Standing in the lobby, I could almost feel Merton's presence.

To gain a firsthand impression of Merton, I interviewed the legendary singer Joan Baez, who had visited Merton at Gethsemani with her friend. When I heard Joan's soft voice on the telephone during our interview, I was mesmerized by her recollections of Merton. She made me laugh when she said that Merton and her friend had been like a couple of drunk Russian convicts after finishing off a bottle of whiskey. Joan adored Merton most after hearing him recount his love for Margie, revealing his very human and flawed dimensions. Weeks later, Joan performed in Columbus, Ohio, on the same day as my sister Anne's birthday. After watching the amazing performance, Lu, her friend Ming-shen and I visited with Joan backstage. Lu would never forget the hug Joan gave her.

During the fall of 2008, as editing on the book continued, I drove with Lu and Black Sox to a library conference in Charleston, South Carolina. We then continued on to Florida to attend the induction of our friend Pete Dye into the World Golf Hall of Fame outside St. Augustine, Florida. And although Pete dazzled the audience with his self-deprecating humor, we all revered him as a genius, one of the greatest golf course architects in the history of the game.

Black Sox loved the trip, playing in the ocean and digging in the warm Florida sand. He had no idea why Lu and I had big smiles on our faces earlier when we had watched a hotel television set in Charleston and learned that Barack Obama had become president. History had been made, and I felt a part of it having gathered signatures for voter registrations in East Lansing. I could also now joke with friends that when they shook my hand, they were shaking the hand that had shaken one of the president's. As a presidential candidate, Obama had appeared in Lansing on his birthday and I had stood in line to see him. After his speech, which was impressive to even those who cared little for his stand on the issues, I walked to the stage to get a closer look. All at once, I noticed he was walking toward me. Like a true groupie, I thrust my hand in the air along with others and when I looked up, I saw him looking directly at me while he shook my hand. It was a priceless moment, and I swore I wasn't going to wash my hand for days. But of course I did.

Despite my belief that East Lansing was to be our home for many years to come since we enjoyed all aspects of living there except for perhaps the cold, snowy, icy winters, I sometimes joked with Lu about her finding a job somewhere warmer like Hawaii. On a cold February 2009 day, I joked about this again. It was then that Lu told me of a job opening at the University of Colorado at Boulder Libraries as a continuing resources cataloger. I was thrilled, not only because of the new challenges that might await her, but because I loved Colorado and my wonderful experiences there. Lu accepted the job after a visit to Boulder for an interview, and we packed Black Sox in the car and headed west. I had never changed the cell phone number I was assigned while living in Aspen before attending seminary, which I considered as yet another sign that the Holy Spirit was working in my life.

In October 2009, our family moved to Superior, a small town outside Boulder, to begin our new life. Needing a place to land, we discovered a huge apartment complex, and applied with the request that our unit be near open space so that Black Sox might enjoy the surrounding trails. When we arrived, and toured our new home, we discovered that out of more than twelve hundred apartments, ours was not only near open space, but had a view, in Aspen's direction, of the Rocky Mountains in all of their glory. On clear days, we were blessed in viewing the orange round ball of sun appear in the east, and in the evenings, watching it disappear beyond the majestic mountain peaks.

Within months, Lu's new position proved itself pleasurable and rewarding, while Black Sox found purpose in barking at the coyotes outside our windows and meeting all sorts of new dog friends during long walks and hikes. I continued mentoring writers who wanted to be published as well as formally consulting with those who wanted help with all aspects of their books. Hearing that one of my clients had become published gave me great satisfaction. In all, a few hundred had experienced the joy of holding a published book in their hands because of our work together.

As the months passed, I discovered the Community United Church of Christ in Boulder that was aligned with my belief that a church should be open to all, including those whose lifestyles may not appeal to everyone. I started attending early morning Sunday Taize services, a combination of prayer, song, and meditation. Through Pastor Peter Terpenning, Lu and I volunteered to help serve the homeless a meal once a month at another church. Interacting with these people, young and old, who were experiencing tough times caused me to pray for them on a daily basis.

In November 2009, during the release of my Merton book, *Beneath the Mask of Holiness: Thomas Merton and the Forbidden Love Affair That Set Him Free*, controversy erupted. For a time, I let myself get caught up in the squabbles between those who enjoyed and were inspired by the book, and those who clearly did not want Merton's human side exposed. The latter, especially those who accused me of being anti-Catholic, forced me into deeper spiritual contemplation and discipline. At times I retreated into my old self, but discovered solace in the many people who wrote to me; those who identified with Merton's personal struggles and connected with the main purpose of the book recognized my tribute to one of the greatest wordsmiths who ever lived, a religious icon who helped me find grace, joy and freedom in my life as he had many others.

The wisdom of Lao-tzu and his work *Tao Te Ching* carried me further along on my path of grace and charity. An ancient Chinese philosopher from the sixth century B.C. whom I discovered while at seminary, Lao-tzu was a contemporary of Confucius. *The Records of the Grand Historian* (circa 100 B.C.) first referenced Lao-tzu and his book *Tao Te Ching:* Tao ("the way"), Te ("virtue in the sense of personal character, inner strength"), and Ching ("great book, classic"). One of my favorite passages is:

> Fame or integrity: which is more important?
> Money or happiness: which is more valuable?
> Success or failure: which is more destructive?
> If you look to others for fulfillment,
> You will never be fulfilled.
>
> If your happiness depends on money,
> You will never be happy with yourself.
> Be content with what you have;
> Rejoice in the way things are.
> When you realize there is nothing lacking,
> The whole world belongs to you.

Discovering how the "world belongs to you" through something call *wu wei*, non-doing or non-action, permits harmony and a feeling of joy without the need for joy, without expectation; those who seek happiness never find it. I wanted my loving and caring for others before myself, as both Christ and Lao-tzu illustrated with their lives, to become second nature. I began practicing "the way" more each day, and slowly but surely, I was, as Merton suggested and Rev. Warren and Lao-tzu confirmed, emptying myself of the old Mark Shaw and letting the new Mark Shaw take over. Lu was an enlightening partner in this quest.

I saw that, more than anything else, I had to overcome my fear, a dreaded enemy. From the moment the troubles in my previous marriage began, ones that would eventually include estrangement from my stepchildren, the ghost of fear chased me. Fear of the unknown then seeped into my psyche. Certainly the human condition is fraught with emotions connected to fear, including disappointment, frustration, stress, anxiety, negativity, worry, anger, and hate, which often reveal themselves through the ego as arrogance, arguably the worst of all human emotions, selfishness and duplicity. We are then led to un-Christlike feelings that initiate deception, alienation, aggression, loneliness, and other regrettable actions. Temptation may be all that we need to make foolish choices, and even though we may know right from wrong, we cannot help ourselves; we are mentally dead, or one step from it, as Thomas Merton elucidated when he spoke about his own self-loathing. The cause of his anxiety, he wrote, was "the mark of spiritual insecurity."

I started to recognize my anger before it could show its ugly head, and as my consciousness evolved, transformed my anger into disappointment, and then into understanding, peace, forgiveness, and soon love, the greatest of all human emotions. According to Merton, we experience love at the "point of nothingness" within our souls where we shine as bright as any diamond ever discovered. Here we are truly One with the Spirit, listening for the true voice of God every waking moment.

Certainly I had died, but now I was alive again. By the spring of 2010, I was convinced that I was the most blessed man on the face of the earth. Could anything exceed what I had experienced over the past few years during my spiritual journey?

CHAPTER TEN

Blessed by a Miracle

During the initial months of living in Colorado for the third time, the Holy Spirit's grace continued to make itself known.

Unlike many other locations across the nation and around the world, people *want* to live in Colorado, especially those who are physically active. Colorado promotes a real free spirit, a love and appreciation of nature and the outdoors, with the cool mountain air brightening each day. There are more than three hundred days of sunshine in the state, a far cry from other parts of the country where the sun rarely shines during the winter months.

Again I became involved with kids in the local community. The Boulder YMCA asked me to coach a fourth-grade boys' basketball team. I watched as youngsters who barely knew how to bounce or shoot a ball when we began the season, became good team players with improved individual skills by the season's end. Since the group had never played together before, we lost the first two games, but then the squad began to take shape and we won the majority of our remaining games. I adored working with the boys and their exceptional parents, all responsible and loving. What coach wouldn't like hearing parents say, "We don't care if they win or lose. Just wear them out!"

Managing a 13- to 15-year-old boys' baseball team, however, was disappointing. Now I saw the bad side of parents, many who were not only absent from games, but did little to ensure their sons' attendance. These kids reflected their parents' poor attitudes with their own poor performances. They didn't give a damn, and I could do little to change their minds.

Coaching the two Colorado teams made me, at sixty-five years old, realize once again that the time for me to be a parent had passed. I would never experience my own child's birth, the diaper days, the cutting of teeth, the crying through the night, the first day of school, or the "terrible twos." I would never help my own son or daughter learn to ride a bike, celebrate a first birthday or any birthdays, read stories at bedtime, buy a first dress, or first sport coat, be there for the first prom, and most of all, hear the words, "I love you, Daddy," or even be called Dad, Daddy, or Father. I was resigned to this, I told myself, and had no regrets. I was grateful for my beautiful and magical life.

To be certain, the toughest times through the years for me had been when someone asked, "How are the triplets doing?" or "How is Kimberly doing?" and I gave some vague answer to cover up the hurt of not knowing how they were doing. I couldn't comment on their weddings since I had not been invited, or tell anyone about their children since I knew nothing. I was especially embarrassed when whoever was questioning me seemed to realize that I was not leveling with them, that I was hiding something, that somehow through my foolish actions, I had lost my family. But those days were behind me, I assured myself, they were gone. Now I lived in

Colorado, and during walks with Black Sox along trails leading to the nearby mountains, I thanked the Holy Spirit again and again for my blessings. I had all a man could ask for, and when I prayed I was careful not to ask for anything more. I had even written two hundred pages of a manuscript for a memoir called *It's Not About You*, which outlined the defining moments in my life through the spiritual journey to seminary and connecting with Lu. But I knew something was missing, an ending to the story perhaps, an unexplained event. With this in mind, I shelved the manuscript in anticipation of what might happen during the ensuing months and years.

On March 16, 2010, as a blazing ball of sun rose further into the clear blue sky against the backdrop of the snowcapped Rocky Mountains, I turned on the computer in my writing studio and began to check e-mail. Black Sox played with his small, blue rubber ball, hiding it under his mangled blanket and then finding it again, something he would repeat for hours on end. After glancing through a large window toward the Flatirons, a rock formation serving as the majestic backdrop for the city of Boulder and beyond, I deleted several nonsense e-mails. Then I clicked on one from a man named James Morrison. He had written to me a couple of days earlier telling me that he was a "fan" of my books. This put a smile on my face since so many had been critical of my writings, which can cause people to stop and think about issues they wanted to avoid. In that e-mail, James wondered whether I had spent some time in Minneapolis, Minnesota in the late 1960s. He told me his mother-in-law had lived there. He wanted to know whether I might have "hung out" with her.

I had written him back stating that yes, I had resided in St. Paul during the late summer and early fall of 1968 and perhaps into the early months of 1969, when I worked as a salesman for a national chemical company. But I told him that I had no recollection of meeting anyone specifically, as that time period was a bit of a blur. When I showed Lu the e-mail, she said, "Ah ha, an old flame." I had expected communication with James to end after our brief exchange the day before, and so was quite surprised to find another of his e-mails in my inbox. Curious, I began to read:

> Mark - Things can certainly become magical! I guess at this point I should lay my cards on the table and tell you the real reason I am writing. I am writing on behalf of my wife.
>
> My wife is a marriage and family therapist and a wonderful mother. We are both people of integrity and professional people with careers we are passionate about. We both come from good families. My wife is adopted. A few years ago she decided to find out about her origins. Going through Lutheran Social Services [in Mpls.] she was able to locate her birth mother.
>
> It has been a positive experience for her. For non-adoptees it is difficult to imagine the haunting feeling of not knowing who you are . . . where you come from . . . and the context of your entry into the world. For my wife half the mystery has now been solved. (She now has a relationship with her biological mother).
>
> However—and this is the "magical part"—her birth mother had extremely limited information about the birth father. She told us the father was unaware of the birth and pregnancy (She even kept the pregnancy hidden from her parents). All she could tell us was that she "dated him briefly" (days), he was a "nice guy," "blonde with blue eyes," "not from the area," some intention/involvement with "law school" with a reference to "Chicago," and his name was Mark Shaw.
>
> To be honest, my wife and I had no real intention of locating her birth father—in part because we did not want to interrupt a person's

life with this kind of knowledge after forty years. But, when I was online looking for books on how to "get published" (I'm writing a play about Uncle Sam) your name came up! I was a bit taken aback with your name, and appearance, and age. My curiosity got the best of me and I initiated contact with you.

My wife was born April 17, 1969. Honestly . . . I don't expect you to "do anything." I just wanted you to know that I could not resist contacting you and maybe finding out if you are "him." I'm sending you two photos. One is of her and I, and the other is of my wife's adoptive family. If you zoom in on her, I think you can see why I saw some similarities with you. She has three brothers. Her [adoptive] father passed away twenty months ago. I really loved the guy! He had a PhD in theology and with my interest in world religion (I teach it), we had endless wonderful discussions!

Well . . . I hope I have not totally freaked you out! You have every right to not respond. I totally understand . . . peace be with you. James.

Staring at the screen, I yelled, "What?" as my heart nearly burst. My fingers could not move fast enough as I hit the keys necessary to download the two photographs James had sent. The first was of James and the woman who might very well be my daughter. They were positioned near a river with a rock formation behind them. James wore sunglasses, but the woman's face was clear. I sighed while noticing the gap between her front teeth, the wavy eyebrows, her nose, and the way her smile spread across her face. Immediately my mind superimposed my face on hers and there was no doubt of an exact duplicate. "Wow!" I shouted loud enough to make Black Sox' ears perk up. "Wow!" again, I yelled.

In the second photograph, James' wife stood third to the right in the back row with the three brothers from her adoptive family. In the front row sat her adoptive parents, each with loving smiles on their faces. The woman was a bit younger looking in the photo, but with her blond hair fashioned more on top of her head than in the other photo, I was drawn to how much she looked like my mother Vera. I gasped at this thought, at how I could see my mom's features so definitively.

Mesmerized, I stared at the two photos time and time again. I simply could not take my eyes off of them, especially the photo of James and his wife; the facial similarities between us were unbelievably evident. For more than an hour, I looked at the photos, read the e-mail again, and then looked at the photos again. Slowly, the full brunt of James' intention became clear: this man who had cleverly pretended to be a "fan" of my books was now telling me he strongly suspected I could very well be the father of his wife, a woman who had never known who her birth father and mother were for nearly four decades.

I became teary-eyed as the impact of James' message hit me upside the head like a two-by-four. I rose from my chair, walked unsteadily toward the living room, and began pacing back and forth like a father awaiting the birth of his daughter, which in essence, I was, even though the "birth" of my daughter might be happening in her fortieth year.

Was this possible, I wondered? Was I about to experience a true miracle in my life? Had the Good Lord, the magical Spirit that had guided my life through many trials and tribulations, sent me a miracle, one beyond imagination? Did I have a daughter, and if this woman had children of her own, was I a grandfather? Could this all be occurring at the age of sixty-five, after such an incredulous life laden with bizarre, mind-boggling experiences, almost more fictitious than factual? Certainly, having been a stepfather was a blessing, but being a biological father would be something even more amazing.

During the hours that followed, my mind raced with thoughts of the possibilities. I wore out the carpet next to the computer with my pacing. What would Lu think of all this, I wondered? She knew I was a crazy, unpredictable man who had changed her lifestyle after we had met five years earlier. But this news . . . unimaginable. My palms were sweaty even thinking about how I would tell Lu. Black Sox sensed my unsteady state, gazing up at me as if to say, "Hey, are you losing it?" I was.

When Lu finally arrived at home from work, she asked what I wanted for dinner. Barely able to speak, and without answering the trivial dinner question, I instead responded that she had better sit down at the computer. I sat down on the couch across from her and asked her to look at the photograph of James and the woman that I had on the screen. I could see her dancing brown eyes surveying the image carefully. (Lu later told me how she thought the woman in the photo was my sister Anne at a younger age, but dismissed the idea when she noticed the contemporary clothing.) Lu looked at me, and then the photo, and back to me again. With a lump in my throat, and tears streaming down my cheeks, I said, "I think that's my daughter." Lu gasped, looked back at the photograph, and then looked at me with a big grin on her face. As I held my breath, she exclaimed, "She looks like you! She has your eyebrows!"

I rose and hugged Lu with all my might. If what James had written was true, I was a father and Lu was a stepmother. Could this be true, could it really be true? Even the thought of it sent shivers through my spine as I attempted to comprehend our news. When I could finally think rationally, one thought was crystal clear: the Holy Spirit had worked wonders to prepare me for this mystical moment, one where I might receive the greatest gift imaginable, the gift of a child, a flesh-and-blood child, a daughter almost out of thin air. Without doubt, I knew for certain, every experience, every defining moment, had led to this discovery, this miracle, this time when being a biological father was now possible instead of impossible.

Dumfounded by this turn of events, Lu and I read James' e-mail over and over again, each time attempting to understand its true meaning. As I did, my mind wandered back to the late sixties when I had spent time in Minnesota. Specifics were vague, but the timing was certainly right for me to have dated James' wife's biological mother (by her request, she wishes to remain anonymous). When we looked closely at the two photographs James had forwarded, one significant characteristic of the woman whose name I did not even know yet was more apparent than any other—her teeth. Zooming in on them, we realized they were an exact duplicate of mine, two large front teeth with a bit of a gap between. And the nose, yes, the nose, was quite similar to mine. And the smile, a broad smile, yes, that was similar as well. And the eyebrows, yes, again, similar. Was this my daughter? Yes, Lu and I were both beginning to believe that it truly was.

To fully consider this startling news, we went out to dinner to decide the best course of action. For the first few minutes at the restaurant, we sat in silence, each of us in deep thought, neither one knowing what to say. Were we really parents? Could this be possible? One day we had no hope of ever being parents; now it suddenly appeared that we were.

James had certainly given me an "out" by explaining that he did not expect me to "do anything," that I did not even have to acknowledge his e-mail and could instead simply move on with my life. Later, a few friends asked why I never considered his offer. I told them such a choice never entered my mind. Not once, because I somehow knew, even knew from the tone and wording of the first two vague e-mails from James, that the Holy Spirit was at work again and I had to be open to whatever It had in store for me.

With these thoughts in mind, and Lu's blessing and love right beside me, I drafted an e-mail immediately upon returning home. Although I became emotional many times, I was able to respond to James rather quickly:

> James - Composing an email response to yours is not an easy thing to do. This day has been filled with many emotions as I read your words over and over again.
>
> First, let me say that based on the timing, and the similarities between your wife and me, there is no doubt in my mind that I am her biological father. For better or worse, she has my teeth structure and other facial features resembling mine. My wife Lu noticed the similarity in the eyebrows as well. Whether she has my dry, sarcastic sense of humor and passion for adventure remains to be seen.
>
> Learning that I am her biological father (I am uncertain as to whether you have told her of your research yet) is a quite proud moment for me. During my only other marriage, I raised four step-children including triplet boys. They were eight when I met them and their sister was ten. For the next thirteen years, I poured my love into their lives as if they were my own children. To know that I have a child of my own is quite special. How blessed I am.

Based on your comments about your wife (you did not provide her name), I am proud to be the father of such a lovely and accomplished woman. It appears that you two have carved out a wonderful life together. And that she was most blessed to have been adopted by a caring family. Hopefully I will meet them one day to thank them personally. It is too bad that I could not have met her father as we both had interests in theology.

I would certainly look forward to meeting my daughter with you and the children if this is what she wants to do. If a telephone call makes sense, please feel free for either of you to call me at our home near Boulder, Colorado. Or if you want me to call, I will do so.

If your wife wants to meet, I would be pleased to do so when it is convenient for both of you. Certainly Lu and I would be willing to fly to Minnesota or we could welcome you here in Colorado. Our home is your home.

By way of recollection, I do recall dating a woman in Minnesota. While our time together in St. Paul may have been short, I believe we kept in touch when I moved to Chicago. This must be how she knew I was considering law school.

Obviously, your finding me through an internet search for publication help was meant to be. These things do not occur accidentally. If I may help you with your publishing aspirations, please let me know.

I thank you for tracking me down. Regardless of what occurs from this point on, you have given me a wonderful gift. I must tell you that for whatever reason, after your first two emails, I had a feeling within me that there was more to this than simple curiosity about my knowing your mother-in-law. Obviously, there was.

I will now await word as to what you feel is the next step. If for whatever reason your wife does not feel it wise to make contact, I will certainly understand. But no matter what, please let her know that I love her.

Blessings and love,
Mark

After sending the message, sleep was impossible. During the night, I reconstructed the chain of events from the moment of James' first communication. I then reexamined the e-mail I had sent to James wondering if it was too much, or too little. Had I said the right things? As I sat on the couch trying to understand what had happened, I wondered if I would ever hear from James again.

The next morning, I had my answer when James responded by thanking me for my willingness to continue the dialogue and for attempting to help solve the mystery evolving day by day. During subsequent e-mails, the essence of the miracle began to unfold as I learned more about the mystical path James had taken to find me, and why there was even more evidence that the Holy Spirit was working overtime to bring my daughter and me together.

First, James e-mailed me that his wife's name is Marni Morrison. During the next few minutes, I simply repeated her name; the name of the woman who James thought was my daughter. I couldn't stop, somehow just wanting to hear her name, to savor the sound of it. Then James hit me with news that made goose bumps travel up and down my arms and legs and tears flood my eyes: Marni had two children, Allison, age seventeen, and Lucy, age ten. This meant that if Marni was my daughter (and I was certain she was), then I had two grand-daughters. I hugged Lu again, for now she was a stepgrandmother, and my parents, bless them in Heaven, were great-grandparents. My brother was an uncle, and my sisters, aunts.

New e-mails elaborated on Marni's work as a family therapist at a Native American reservation near Red Wing, and that James had furthered his research about me on various Internet sites. He also disclosed that at one point a couple of years earlier, he had tracked down a Mark Shaw in Champaign, Illinois based on the birth mother's information that the Mark Shaw they were looking for might be practicing law there, but the Mark Shaw practicing law in Illinois would have only been six years old in 1968.

With each passing day, I could not even imagine what was going through Marni's mind, but I prayed for her, and hoped she was handling well the anticipation of learning whether I could be her father. Lu said that based on the information from Marni's mother and her sister, and the similarities in appearance, it would now be more of a surprise if I *weren't* Marni's father than if I were. I agreed, especially since James told me that in the whole of the United States, there were only 836 "Mark Shaws" over the age of thirteen. What were the odds of my not being the father in lieu of all of the evidence pointing my way? Slim to none, I believed.

To prove the father/daughter relationship beyond any doubt, per Marni's request, and before Marni and I began to communicate directly, it was decided through James that a paternity test was in order. I gladly made arrangements for my test in Colorado, and she was set for a test in Minnesota. Imagine, a sixty-five-year-old guy like me taking a paternity test, and *wanting* it to be positive, which was the case as I ambled anxiously one early March morning into a testing lab not far from our home. When I told the receptionist I was there for a paternity test, she seemed a bit bewildered. She chuckled when I asked her if I was the oldest fellow to take such a test. Then a nurse handed me a document where I added my signature above the title "Alleged Father," which made me chuckle.

As we awaited the results, Marni and I exchanged e-mails for the first time, an experience that was, to be certain, surreal. I had to stop and consider that this was my daughter I was e-mailing with, not some stranger as she shared the defining moments in her life. After her birth in Minneapolis, she was adopted by Gary and Mary Peterson. They had three biological sons, Paul, Erik, and Marcus, and a daughter Mary Janice who died at the age of two in the early 1960s. Following Marni's adoption, the family spent four years in Scotland where Gary earned a PhD in theology, and then returned to Minnesota.

Each day, I woke and raced to the computer to learn more about Marni. She told me that her memories of the early years, especially after she learned she was adopted, were filled with excitement and also struggle as she questioned her identity and genealogy, wondering why she had been put up for adoption. She told me that one of her brothers teased her about "being bought and paid for." But she felt confident about the love between her and her brothers, describing the fun they had shared throughout the years.

Oftentimes, when she was growing up, Marni said she wondered if she were "bad" whether her parents would send her back to the adoption services, or back to where she had lived for the first six months of her life, which was still a mystery to everyone. Curious about how Marni might feel about her adoption caused me to read anything I could find about adoptees and the emotions they encounter through the years, including *The Primal Wound: Understanding the Adopted Child* by Nancy Newton Verrier. Much of the discussion in the book revolves around abandonment issues, as most adoptees struggle with one main question: "Why would my mother, and father if he knew of the birth, decide to give me up for adoption?" The book also addresses other topics, such as the fear of rejection, issues of trust and intimacy, and guilt, shame, and identity. Of these, the question of identity resonated with me most. I tried to imagine how Marni felt as she questioned her true identity when she did not know who her biological parents were. Did she have any medical history worth noting? Did she have to leave lines blank when she was asked about it?

The next day, in an e-mail on March 17, James had touched on how Marni had felt over the years:

> My, oh my. What a day it has been for all of us. OK . . . here's the deal . . . Marni is happy AND eager to solve this—it has been a haunting mystery for her ALL her life. And given your beautiful and sensitive response to my email she is honestly hoping it is YOU and that you will get a chance to get to know her and your grandchildren . . .

I responded with some hope of continuing to keep things on the light side:

> [Lu and I] are both rather in a daze but each of us has a smile on our face . . . If Marni is not my daughter, especially in lieu of the information provided by her birth mother and the similarities previously mentioned, then I will, to use an odd expression, eat cheese through a paper plate. Not sure what that means as I just made it up.

A day later, I stared at the computer screen and blinked when I saw the e-mail from my daughter. It was an e-mail from Marni in response to one I had sent her, one filled with *Wows* over the sudden turn of events. She replied:

WOW is right. It seems as if my loving husband has 'gotten the ball rolling,' so to speak, without me. I have to admit, I am quite overwhelmed. Does this picture help? My birth mother was a student back in 1968 at the U. of M. Interior design I believe . . . Didn't Hemingway say something about courage being grace under pressure? So here we go.

When Lu and I looked at the photograph of Marni's birth mother at about age twenty-one or so, I definitely recognized something about her. She was a pretty girl with flowing blond hair. Why she had taken an interest in a character like me I did not know, but I was thankful she had done so. I certainly regretted not recalling more about her.

Awaiting the results of the paternity test was excruciating for everyone. Every time the telephone rang, I wondered if this was *the* call telling me whether my status as "alleged father" would change to "real father." There was little question in my mind since the age was right, the timing of my stint in Minnesota coincided (1968), and the similarities in appearance were undeniable. James had even superimposed half of my face from a website photograph above a link to my Wikipedia page with half of Marni's, and there was little doubt the facial features matched perfectly. He had also checked my birth date, which revealed that I was indeed twenty-three years old in 1968.

James then forwarded a photograph of Kastina and Jarek, his two biological children from his previous marriage, alongside Marni's daughters, Allison and Lucy. Seeing the faces of the two girls, the two girls who were in all likelihood my granddaughters, made me shout "Thank you, Lord!" so loud Black Sox scampered out of the room. On the day the physical photographs arrived, I looked at them a thousand times with glistening eyes. I was trembling with happiness.

When I glanced again at the photograph of Marni's adoptive family that James had sent, I was pleased to see the content look on her face as she stood in the back with her brothers. I also noticed how peaceful her father Gary looked in the photo. James and Marni explained that Gary had passed away twenty months earlier and how much they missed him. I only wish I had known him before he died so I could have thanked him for being a wonderful father to the child, and later woman, I believed to be my daughter.

As the days passed by without any test results, James, Marni, and I traded information about athletic skill (and my lack thereof with regard to swimming); eye color (mine are off-blue, same as Marni's); hair color (she wondered whether I had a trace of red in mine at an earlier age—I had); Marni's first contact with the adoption service in 1999 in search of health information after her daughter Lucy's birth; my passion for Roy Orbison songs; James' love of nature and the mountains and his recollections of visiting nearby Rocky Mountain National Park as a youngster; and their nonstop drive to Key West where they enjoyed Captain Tony's, the bar where my favorite author Ernest Hemingway had written some of his book text while tipping a few.

In another jaw-dropping moment, Marni told me that, at a young age, she had been told that her birth father was dead. In explanation of my supposed death, she wrote on March 22:

> So you want to know how you (if you are you) died? Hahaha . . . Well, I was told at a young age that you died in a motorcycle accident. And then the story was confirmed by Lutheran Social Services when Lucy was a couple months old. I called them

wanting medical information about the both of you. Before the letter arrived confirming my birth mother's clean bill of health I got a phone call from an LSS worker named Jackie worried that I didn't know you were dead, wanting to tell me in person.

Then, later in my life, I suppose about 7 years ago or so . . . Jim and I decided to get the "full file" of my story. Without names however . . . there . . . written eloquently . . . was "your story." It went that you and my birth mother were in love, plans of marriage, and that you were a pre-med student. Your Father was a doctor and started a clinic in some third world country. Your mom was a stay at home mother and I think you had a few siblings. (I have the original letter around . . . I'll find it for you!) Anyway, you suddenly died in an accident. The letter stated that both your parents and my birth mother's wanted to take me in and raise me . . . but my birth mother decided adoption was the best route.

Three years ago . . . in one of the first phone conversations with my birth mother . . . she asked how "my parents" were dealing with me finding/meeting her. I said that my mother was struggling, but my dad was fine. Probably because my birth father was dead . . . no threat . . . she then blurted out "Your dad's not dead! His name is Mark Shaw and he's a lawyer in Champaign, Illinois!" I proceeded to hit my head on the wall behind the bed where I was sitting as I threw my head back in shock. I talked about this new news with my parents later that night . . . who at the time . . . lived down the road. Mark, I can't even remember how my dad reacted. I miss him. That's why I have to keep you at arm's length until we know for sure.

You have so many similarities that it chills me. My mom and dad adopted me when I was 6 months old . . . no one knows where I was for those 6 months. One of the mysteries I suppose.

. . . Anyway, when I was a year old, we moved to Scotland. We lived there for 4 years while my dad was at the University getting his

Ph.D. in theology. Weird . . . he was a ELCA pastor in Eden Prairie, MN for years after that . . . and when I was in High School . . . ran for Mayor and held for three terms. After that, he was a missionary in Mexico City through the ELCA church.

You responded like him, you look like him, you joke like him . . . weird and wow indeed! Anyway . . . back to your question. My birth mother tells the story. She met you through her sister. You were a friend of a friend . . . met at a party I believe . . . you were a good guy . . . good looking and smart. Brief encounter . . . then the story ends. The only other persons that knew she was pregnant was her sister and a friend.

"Wow, and wow again," I wrote to her as tears filled my eyes in sympathy with the rocky road she had traveled before James had tracked me down. Certainly the chances of my being Marni's father were huge. Any other verdict was simply not possible. I knew it would break both of our hearts.

Regarding my being "dead," Marni explained that her birth mother believed the letter in the adoption file was a "lie" and written by someone other than her. The truth about the letter didn't matter to me. I was alive, and the Holy Spirit had prepared me for this point in time. Now all we needed was DNA confirmation from the paternity test. Although the wait was excruciating, I used the time to learn more about Marni and her job helping Native Americans with what she called "therapeutic practice"—"basically keeping kids safe, but with their families" at Prairie Island Indian Reservation. She also told me about the family dog, Lyle. My ears perked up as Lyle had been the name of my sister Anne's late husband.

Directing my attention to past struggles, Marni mentioned her familiarity with the Bob Knight war. She wrote, "From what I can gather regarding your run-in with Bob Knight . . . mind you I don't know the specifics . . . but bravo!" Marni also discussed her daughters, writing, "I can't wait to tell you about your granddaughters. They are such fantastic individuals." I replied, "Re Allison and Lucy, just hearing the word 'granddaughters' was mind-boggling. How blessed I would be to be able to meet them and know them."

Wanting to be completely open about my relationship with my stepchildren, I wrote:

> You should know that I do not have much of a relationship with my step-children. Whatever their mother told them during the divorce caused a separation and though I have attempted reconciliation many times, it has not worked out. Am I disappointed? Yes. But somehow, I believe, whatever Spirit guides me along decided to end that chapter of my life, and I look back at my nearly thirteen years with them with positive feelings all around. I pray for them every day and hope they are doing well.

Marni replied:

> As for your step-children . . . those things do happen. I didn't want to ask, but had gotten that feeling. I'm sure they know you are there for them if they should need you. That might be comfort enough, and possibly less stressful for everyone.

The next day I learned that Marni, James, Allison, and Lucy lived in a high-ceilinged loft in downtown Red Wing, having downsized from their larger previous home. Lucy spent half of her time with her father Rob, and half with Marni and James. James' parents, Leon and Audrey, whom Marni told me treated the girls as their own granddaughters, lived nearby on a nice-sized farm east of Red Wing in Wisconsin. Apparently James and Marni helped with the farm work during the summers when James, a high school teacher and creator of an innovative yet controversial world religion course, was not teaching school. When Leon, the farmer, saw the photographs showing the gapped tooth similarity, he jokingly said there had to be a match due to the biological marker, one similar to that with cattle or horses.

On April 6, the drama continued as Marni e-mailed that she had learned the test results were completed and now only subject to review by the lab testing director the following day. I tossed and turned during the night, and kept Lu from resting comfortably.

The next day, attention to my new book, a fresh study of the JFK assassination, waned as I waited for the telephone to ring. Finally, I decided that if I waited all day for the call, it would never come. So I left the apartment and sure enough, when I returned, there was a voice mail awaiting me. With my fingers nearly numb and my heart racing at Mach 10 speed, I dialed the number only to learn that the woman with the results was out to lunch. Then I checked e-mail and read James' message on April 7, 2010, a day that I will never forget.

James wrote:

Mark – Marni is overwhelmed!!!! She is leaving work as we speak. She needs time to process this— so many conflicting emotions and feelings! We will be in touch, but she now needs some time to absorb all this. If she seems 'distant', do not take it personally!!!!! Right now we need to get through the day! You are my father-in-law and you have grandchildren and a WONDERFUL daughter!!!! WOW!!!!"

The "wow" I screamed must have rattled windows for blocks on end. Black Sox jumped to his feet as if a coyote was approaching. I stood up, clapped my hands, and shouted "Wow!" again followed by "I am a father. I am a grandfather. Lu is a grandmother. I have a new son-in-law. My parents are great grandparents. My two sisters and brother have a new niece and two new grand nieces. Amazing. Amazing. Amazing!"

CHAPTER ELEVEN

The Miracle Continues

As I read James' message again and again, especially the words, "you have grandchildren and a WONDERFUL daughter!!!!," a million thoughts crossed my mind.

I thought of the sixties, a time of freedom and revolution. It was the era of rock music at its finest, with Jim Morrison and the Doors leading the way, when there was little concern for political correctness or tradition. As long as people did not hurt others, they were free to do what they pleased. Morrison perhaps summed up the feeling when he said, "This is the strangest life I have ever lived." Yes, it was a strange time, a mellow time for some, and for some, a time to fight for one's beliefs, as the war in Vietnam raged away.

Because her name was Lucy, I had learned that my youngest grandchild (how I enjoyed saying those words over and over again!) loved the Beatles and that her favorite song was "Lucy in the Sky with Diamonds." Our mutual admiration for John, Paul, Ringo and George made me feel especially connected to her and I recalled the first time I saw them on the Ed Sullivan Show in 1964.

When I thought about my other granddaughter Allison soon entering college, I recalled the first days I set foot on the Purdue campus. Upper classmen made us wear green beanies; I looked like a surefire dork. Now my oldest grandchild (there is that word again) would be a freshman. I'd bet she wouldn't tolerate wearing a dumb beanie.

When time permitted reflection, so many "what ifs" confounded me as I considered this dream come true. I was a father and a grandfather all at once. Thank goodness for more liberal laws permitting open access to adoption files in states such as Minnesota. Otherwise, Marni, through James, would have never found her birth mother or me.

Once my parenthood was confirmed, I thought about Lu and her reaction to the news. Five years earlier, she had been living quite peacefully in an apartment near the MSU campus in East Lansing content with her life and work. For more than four years, she had mourned the loss of her beloved husband, Juergen. Then I had to come along with Black Sox and changed her world. Before she knew it, she was married to a wild man who took her on three cross-country trips and off to Europe on a whim. Due partly, I was sure, to my influence, she had given up the safety of a secure position at MSU for a new position at CU. Her life had become a flurry of change, and now she was a stepmother, and a stepgrandmother. She half-jokingly said, "I wonder how many more children will be popping up." I blushed. After all, it was the sixties when free love abounded.

I also considered the new responsibilities of my being a father and grandfather. It was one thing to have been a stepfather, but quite another to have my own child and grandchildren. What were my responsibilities? What would be expected of me? Could I handle it? Should I get some training? Counseling?

On the day of the blessed DNA results, I read a brief e-mail from Marni asking, "You there?" I replied:

> So proud, Marni, to be your father. I certainly wish I had known earlier and could have shared the past years with you, but apparently that was not to be. But now we have the years ahead to get to know each other. A true blessing. I am truly the most blessed man on the face of the earth in so many ways. And even more blessed to have you as my daughter.

Before Marni could reply, James wrote:

> Utterly amazing. Marni did pull herself together and remained at work. I'm not even sure if you heard the official number from the DNA place. Here it is: 99.99 percent confirmation. People have been sentenced to life in prison for less than that I would imagine. Welcome to the family.

As I read these words, I began sobbing, again. But now what? Should I call her? Would she call me? What was the right thing to do? Finally, we decided that she would call me, but as the evening wore on I told Lu this might be difficult for her. My instincts were right as we learned later that Marni kept picking up her cell phone with the intention to call, but then lost the courage to dial. She told me later, "I wanted to call, but I just couldn't. What would you be like? What would we say?"

Now my fingers were trembling as I dialed Marni's number. Twice I touched the wrong key, and had to start over. Finally, I heard the ring and then her voice for the first time. "Hi there," she said. It was truly a miraculous moment, one all of my experiences over the past few years had prepared me for. Then she said, "Wow, you sound pretty good for a dead guy." We both laughed. I realized then that Marni had apparently inherited my strange sense of humor.

Marni and I talked for more than three hours that night. Her voice was crisp, and fresh. It reminded me of my sister Anne's especially when she spoke so assuredly about everything, so directly, so confidently. I could tell she was excited, as excited as I was.

We touched on so many subjects I could never recall them all, but several times I had to remind myself that the woman I was talking to was indeed my daughter, my own flesh and blood. No words can describe this feeling: that I was a father, a real father, talking to a daughter, a real daughter, of mine.

Throughout the conversation, emotion overwhelmed us both as we traded information and tried to catch up on forty years of our lives. At one point, there was silence and then James got on the line. He said Marni had started crying when I told her we had already framed photographs of James and her, the four children, and her and her adoptive family on my writing studio wall. I also told her we had purchased some gifts in Arizona during our visit there two weeks earlier since I was certain she was my daughter. Hearing this, I heard Marni cry again.

After receiving the okay from James and Marni, Lu and I immediately booked tickets to fly to Minnesota the following weekend to celebrate her 41st birthday and Allison's prom night. The next morning, I read an e-mail from her that she had written the night before. She wrote, "Thank you for being you. Thank you for the wonderful chat! Thank God you are alive. Sweet dreams. Love, your daughter Marni." Yes, more tears followed as I used up a last box of Kleenex.

Our conversation had taken place on Wednesday evening, April 7. To our surprise, when Lu and I arrived home on Thursday night from a practice for the youth baseball team I was coaching, the answering machine voicemail light was illuminated. When we listened to the message, we were dumbfounded; it was Marni asking us whether it would be alright for her and James to leave that very moment and drive thirteen hours nonstop to see us in Colorado. If I needed any more proof that Marni was my daughter, this remarkable offer to take a road trip confirmed it. We soon discovered that driving nonstop to places near, and far, was a Morrison—and before that a Peterson—family given. In recent years, Marni and James had driven thirty-three hours straight to Key West from Minnesota. And to New Orleans. And to St. Augustine, Florida, as well.

Lu and I said "yes" in an instant. After a restless night's sleep, I sat on our balcony gazing at the mountains and wondered what it was going to be like when I saw my daughter for the first time. I thought of all my years hoping that I might be a real dad, all the years believing that I would never be. Then, bang, it had happened, the miracle of miracles, three miracles in fact: Marni, Allison and Lucy. I was an instant father, an instant grandfather.

After an anxious wait, I answered the telephone on that magnificent morning of April 9. I heard Marni's voice telling me she was nearby. Since our home was difficult to locate, we had agreed to meet at, of all places, a Conoco gas station three miles away. On the drive there, I looked at Lu and she looked at me as we held hands. Even Black Sox in the backseat seemed to know this was a special occasion.

After pulling into the gas station, I stood by the car looking near and far, my hands wet with sweat. Then a Volkswagen Jetta drove up toward us as Black Sox peered out the window. Five seconds later,

Marni walked toward me, her blonde hair waving in the wind. I hugged my daughter, my very own biological daughter, for the first time. I told her, "I don't want to ever let you go."

When we finally parted, Marni and Lu hugged. Then James and I hugged. Then James and Lu hugged. Hugs all around. I thanked James again for finding me, for making the miracle possible. Later, he told me that Marni made him drive around a bit before they went to the gas station. She was as nervous as I was.

For a few seconds, Marni and I just looked at each other, both trying to figure out what to do next. She was so beautiful, her eyes gleaming, her smile so warm and loving. Then she walked to our car and petted Black Sox for the first time. Our new family rejoiced, together for the first time.

For all of that day and the next, we laughed and talked and laughed some more. Many times, I had to stop and acknowledge that the woman sitting across from me was flesh and blood, that part of my genes were part of her genes, that this was truly my daughter. I watched her facial expressions, noted the similarities, and stared intently at our most striking characteristic, our gapped teeth. Thank goodness neither one of us had a dentist correct this feature. When I examined her overall appearance, I could easily see resemblances to my older sister Anne; they had the same slight build and the same type of voice. I also noted the facial similarities to my mother, Vera, who, along with Dad, must be smiling down from Heaven. When we looked at my mother's photograph together, we all recognized the similarities.

The whole time spent with Marni and James, a stout fellow with a ready smile, and a rock in Marni's life, became a blur, but I know we dined together, drove into Boulder to stroll along the Pearl Street pedestrian mall where Marni held my hand, and visited nearby Eldorado Canyon State Park, home of one of the most accessible rock climbing areas in the world where we watched climbers spider up the steep cliffs as we attempted to savor the meaning behind our new lives. On a trail overlooking the rushing South Boulder Creek, James and Lu took the first photograph of Marni, sitting on a small boulder, and me, beaming while sitting right behind her.

For me, it was truly the culmination of a spiritual journey that had led me from the depths of Hell after the Knightmare toward enlightenment and the current miracle. And to a state of mind where I could truly appreciate the gift I had been granted by the Holy Spirit.

During this trip, Marni and James attended one of my baseball team's games. After it was over, Skylar, an assistant coach, approached us. For the first time in my life, I said, "This is my daughter Marni," beyond thrilled to introduce her as my daughter. Wow, and wow again. When I sat on the deck of our home later that evening, I reflected on the day's events. The old cliché about this being too good to be true came to mind. But it was true, every last bit of it.

Before Marni and James left, there was a moment when I glanced across the room with the full realization that Marni was my daughter. Overcome with emotion, I simply threw my hands in the air and shouted, "This is ******* amazing!" I immediately apologized for using crude language, but Marni, James and Lu were all laughing at my sincerity.

One week later, Lu and I flew to Minnesota and met Allison and Lucy, and other members of Marni's family. When Lu and I arrived at the Minneapolis airport, Marni and two of her brothers, Paul and Erik were waiting for us. We had a great time talking about the past and how James had found me. Later, when Marcus and his family visited us at Marni's home, we listened to him tell stories about their childhood and how they teased and tormented Marni at times. He even admitted to telling a judge "no" at age four when asked whether he wanted a baby sister. I watched Marni to see if Marcus's recollection hurt her, but it appeared she had let that go. He was young at the time, and she had since forgiven him for his resistance to her addition to their family.

I had spoken briefly to both Allison and Lucy on the telephone, but nothing matched the hugs I experienced from them both during our two-day stay in Red Wing. I was impressed with their beauty and poise. Allison was celebrating her high school senior prom night. I felt so proud standing next to her while she wore the most dazzling black and white gown. She stole the show when the prom dates paraded around the high school gymnasium. And Lucy—wow—my heart nearly exploded with joy when she walked across the living room and sat next to me on the couch. She cuddled up to me like a teddy bear and I held her tight while admiring her smile, like Allison's, that could light up any room.

Concordant with everything else about the miracle, the timing of the visit permitted Lu and me to celebrate Marni's forty-first birthday with her. I may have missed the first forty, but I would never miss one again.

We gave Marni several presents, among them framed photographs of my mother and father and me at about the age when I would have lived in Minnesota. Thanks to my family members, we had many photographs of my grandfather and even great-great-grandfather and great-great-grandmother to show Marni, James, and the girls. We met their dog Lyle and presented him with a rawhide bone.

Most touching was learning that my sisters Anne and Debbie, and Anne's daughter Julie, had sent Marni birthday cards. Debbie later told Marni about how the joy of my discovery had brought my extended family even closer together. Each had been so happy for me, especially as they had witnessed the depth of sorrow I experienced during the Knightmare and the subsequent divorce.

Before Allison's prom, we drove to James' parents' farm where we watched his father Leon call the cattle. As if by magic, each cattle (not cow, Leon informed me) immediately headed toward Leon from a hundred yards away, despite their peaceful state. I stood with Lucy as cattle named "Demon" and "Ruth" ate hay out of our hands. James' mother Audrey then accompanied us to my granddaughter Allison's pre-prom parade. People must have wondered why I was constantly smiling.

During our visit, I talked on the telephone with Mary, Marni's adoptive mother. I could tell she was quite pleased that Marni, through James, had found me. I thanked her and Gary for having raised such a remarkable woman. I made a promise that when I finally met her, she and I would have a long chat so that she knew how much I appreciated her raising Marni. Mary and Gary had given Marni love when I wasn't around; to me they were saints, guardian angels, sent from Heaven to take care of my daughter until she could find me.

During the subsequent weeks after the miracle occurred, Marni and I talked and e-mailed and became closer as we got to know each other better. Each day I learned a bit more about her and the life she had led prior to our meeting.

On the eighteenth of May, Marni sent an e-mail that made my whole body shake with joy. In part, she wrote:

Even though most of our lives we have been apart, you have a calming way about you that makes me feel very at home and truly loved … The way you care about Lu and your special dog Black Sox, that you coach kids, that you care about your friends, and that you take time to celebrate the special and wonderful things in life. Even if it's a cloud. I love that you write positive notes on your hand, that you don't eat gray/brown food. I love that you swear, that you're sarcastic and that you poke fun at yourself, not others.

Marni then added,

I love that you partied in the past, that you celebrate a crazy man like Hemingway and that you love to travel. Love that you think out of the box, that you challenge people's thoughts and truths, and that you have looked at and faced your own . . . I love how when you are talking with a person, they have your undivided attention. I love that you hug, smile and laugh freely. I love that you appreciate nature and the spirit. I love that you make people feel important, especially how you have blessed me, James and your granddaughters. With that, my dear, I call you Dad. Please know that you are loved for exactly who you are.

Hearing these loving words from my daughter was just about more than I could take. I read them a hundred times over and then pinned the e-mail to the wall by my writing table. The Spirit had not only let me feel the emotions of having a daughter, but one who was exceptionally caring and wonderful. I just sat and stared at the e-mail as the hours passed. How incredibly blessed I was. When I prayed that day, tears kept interrupting my thoughts. I was becoming a crybaby and I didn't care. The love of a daughter—is there anything more precious in life?

In early June, I flew to Minnesota to attend Allison's high school graduation. I looked forward to meeting Mary and others in my new family. When I met Mary and hugged her for the first time, I repeated my thanks to her for raising Marni, and told her how much I wished I had met Gary. She had collected some unique photographs of Marni during her early years and gave them to me.

On the flight back to Colorado and over the next few days, I never quit thinking about my new moniker as a father and grandfather, how I would experience a true Father's Day in every sense of the word, how my genes would survive. How far they would stretch into the future was unknown, but if either Allison or Lucy had children, then my genes would live into the future. This meant a great deal to me as it would any father, and I was so thankful for the grace the Good Lord had shown me. Friends and my sister Anne explained my miracle as a true gift from the Lord as solace for my lost contact with my stepchildren. I wasn't certain if they were right. All I was certain about was that I had been blessed in so many ways in my life, but nothing compared to this.

Being a father and grandparent means keeping photographs in a wallet and proudly showing them to anyone and everyone. It means saying things like, "I'm sorry I can't have lunch because I have to shop for birthday presents for my grandkids." It means telling others, "Oh, my daughter is a family therapist. I will ask her about the problem you have." It means asking others what they might suggest buying for a grandchild's high school graduation present. It means worrying a bit when your daughter doesn't call as expected, or you hearing that your grandchild has a cold and missed school. It even means being able to check the box on a questionnaire in the doctor's office when it asks about offspring; the first time I responded "Marni Morrison" in the space below, my hand trembled as I wrote the words.

Being a father made me feel ten feet tall, made me want to tell every father to savor fatherhood and savor the time spent with his children. I wanted to shout as loud as possible: love them every single moment of your life, and let them know you love them. In the grand scheme of things, being a father and grandfather was impacting every part of my life, changing everything. I continued to learn day by day. My only regret was that my parents did not have the opportunity to meet Marni, Allison, Lucy and our new family. But I knew for certain they had to be smiling from Heaven above.

If this had been a miracle for me, it had certainly been one for Marni as well. For more than thirty-five years of her life, she had no idea who either of her birth parents were. She admitted that having no roots of her own left a hole in her heart. Learning about her birth mother began to fill that hole. Marni also now knew why she was put up for adoption; that she had done nothing wrong, that her birth mother had chosen to continue the pregnancy, yet aware as a young, unsettled woman, she wasn't prepared to raise a child alone. Marni could now understand and accept her adoption, and appreciate her loving, caring adoptive parents whom she still called Mom and Dad. I was the biological father, but in her heart I knew Marni would always view Gary as her father, as she should. Like a stepfather, an adoptive father is critically important to a child, which I empathized with naturally. But learning the identity of both her biological parents provided some closure for Marni, and infinite pleasure for me. As Lu and I told Marni, she is stuck with us and we will be there for her and the girls for the rest of our lives.

However, I still couldn't grasp why the miracle happened, and why it occurred at the time it did in Marni's life. When I reviewed the defining moments in brief detail—birth, adoption, early and high school years with her adoptive parents by her side, college days, marriage to John and the birth of Allison, divorce, single motherhood while earning her undergraduate degree and working full time, marriage to Rob and the birth of Lucy, earning a master's degree, divorce from Rob and marriage to James, locating her birth mother, adoptive father Gary's death and then James tracking me down (emotional rollercoaster moments all around)—one could come up with all sorts of theories as to the timing of James locating me. Certainly Marni had shown courage throughout her life dealing with all sorts of obstacles. As a strong-minded woman, I could visualize her searching for and finding her birth parents at any of those trying periods, despite any potential for disappointment. So why at this point in time?

We can never know a Higher Power's whole purpose for us, but this perplexing series of events made me consider how the two worlds of Marni and Mark finally collided. On my side, I am convinced that this Spirit was preparing me for the miracle. I had to suffer difficult times, especially with the breakup of my marriage after the Bob Knight fiasco and the separation from my stepchildren, in order to grow by embarking on a spiritual journey that took me back to Aspen, then to seminary in California, to falling in love and marrying Lu, to East Lansing, and then to Colorado. Finally, it would seem, with me a bit settled, perhaps this Spirit decided the time was right to present me with the greatest gift one may imagine, the gift of a lifetime: a child. Certainly if this would have happened years ago, I would not have been ready for it. But I was ready now. Quite ready, especially with Lu, the light of my life, beside me to share the miracle.

For Marni, one may only guess why this miracle occurred during her fortieth year. Perhaps it was telling that after she and James received information that I was not dead as previously believed, Gary's illness prevented them from following up. If Gary were still alive, and of course, I wished he still were, then maybe this whole miracle would have been more complicated. Maybe whatever Higher Power guiding our lives believed that since Marni's beloved father had died, it would present her with a new father in me. All this is speculation, but there is nothing wrong with the unknown as long as we embrace it without fear.

Regarding Marni's birth mother, I will always have a special place in my heart for her. We had a brief time together and then I left for Chicago and law school. She made a brave and hopeful decision giving life to Marni, and then arranging for her adoption. I didn't know, based on several factors, if she and I would ever connect in the future, but she is as much a part of our daughter as I am, and I wished her only the very best.

I wondered about the influence of the miracle on Allison and Lucy. Both had grown up never knowing who their maternal biological grandparents were. Each had a void in their lives, unlike their friends who had known more about their heritage. Now, instead of feeling different from their friends, they knew who their grandparents were on their mother's side, and could hopefully enjoy new relationships with both. For Allison, I could see the change happening as she turned eighteen, while Lucy, whose facial features resembled mine including the gapped teeth, was but eleven. Now they both had Lu and me to love them along with other family members, including Lucy's dad Rob, a stand-up guy who adopted Allison after his marriage to Marni. When Rob and Marni later separated, they showed Lucy and Allison that even through divorce, parents can remain friends.

For some mystical reason that James probably doesn't even understand, he decided to write a stage play. He told Lu and me that he embarked on the idea when Marni accepted a part-time job as a chef at a local restaurant. To occupy himself while she worked on the weekends, he sat in a booth and wrote his Uncle Sam play. Then, because he wanted information on how to publish it, he decided to elicit guidance, and stumbled upon me and my photo.

Miracles are defined simply by Merriam-Webster as "an extraordinary occurrence that is ascribed to a divine or supernatural cause." Pretty simple really, and whether divine or supernatural, what happened was a true gift in every sense of the word. A former colleague of mine, Squire Rushnell, describes such occurrences in his best-selling book, *When God Winks*. He believes, "seemingly random events are actually signposts that can help [people] successfully navigate careers, relationships and interests." In my case, God certainly "winked" at me providing a magical relationship I never thought possible.

The miracle sent to me, and to Marni, James, Allison, Lucy, Marni's birth mother, Mary, and all of those who have shared in its glory, has released a gushing roar of the most important emotion known to mankind: love. Through the reunion, a special father/ daughter relationship had been born, a relationship like no other. It may have come more than forty years after Marni's birth, but it was nevertheless real, and solid, and never ending. No one can ever tear the bond apart; no one can ever take back the miracle. Marni and I both had experienced the emotions of abandonment, albeit on different levels, and now together we could help each other move forward instead of dwelling on the past.

While my life journey to the point of this miracle was filled with potholes—truly the good, the bad, and the ugly—I have learned that the emotion of love has no equal. If we love instead of hate, if we love while forgiving, if we simply "become love" as Thomas Merton suggested, anything is possible in life. While I truly love my wife, and others close to me, my love for my daughter Marni is like no other I will ever experience; fatherhood, and yes, motherhood, is truly the purest form of love. Marni e-mailed me one day in April after a wonderful chat the night before:

> I am truly blessed to have you and Lu in my life. You make me feel complete and I thank you for that. You could have easily chosen not to respond to James's email. I'm so glad you did . . . Truly you are a long awaited blessing. The journey I have been on for the last 40 years now has more meaning than ever.

I could only reply, "Thank you, Lord." Marni's mention of me making her feel "complete" reminded me of Thomas Merton's words about how Margie Smith had prompted a similar emotion in him, and how he felt free because of his love for, and from, Margie. Having Lu in my life, and then Marni and the girls, made me feel free as well, free from the discontent of losing contact with my stepfamily, free from the ties that bound me to the Knightmare.

CHAPTER TWELVE

The Reflections of Fatherhood

During some quiet time a few days after I learned that Marni was my daughter, Black Sox and I roamed a trail near our Superior, Colorado home. A multitude of emotions ran through me. Several times I had to retrieve a red handkerchief from my back pocket and dab moisture from my eyes. Being alone with nature while staring at the majesty of the Rockies made me reflect in depth over the miracle that had entered my life.

During my sixty-five-plus years, I was continually amazed at the experiences allowed a moderately talented man. Certainly I had not been great at anything, and I had been awful at some things. The word "mediocre" described me perfectly. Regardless, I had lived my life to the fullest, and yet there was so much time still ahead of me. But even if I had died that day, it would not have made any difference for I was "ready to step across the line," as Thomas Merton told several of his Gethsemani students, "without any unfinished business." Now I had a daughter, two granddaughters, a son-in-law, and new family members to love and enjoy along with my beloved Lu, and of course, Black Sox.

Maybe Gonzo journalist Hunter S. Thompson had people like me in mind when he wrote, "Who is the happier man, he who has braved the storm of life, or he who has stayed securely on the shore, and merely existed?" Certainly I had not "stayed securely on the shore" in any sense of the word. I had taken chances, tried new things, failed miserably at times, but never backed away from opportunity.

Perhaps one day when I pass into the next world, the Good Lord will explain why I have been blessed in so many ways. Certainly I had been a scoundrel at times, a sinner, one who made many regrettable mistakes. Now I was surrounded by love on every side.

"There is no greater power in the Universe than the power of love," Rhonda Byrne writes in her best-selling book, *The Secret*, reinforcing my perception of the magical persuasion of love. She adds, "The feeling of love is the highest frequency you can emit. If you could wrap every thought in love, if you could love everything and everyone, your life would be transformed . . . Thought impregnated with love becomes invincible."

Our search for love is universal. Thomas Merton, during the time when he discovered true love's meaning, wrote these words in my favorite book of his, *New Seeds of Contemplation*: "Love is my true identity. Love is my true character. Love is my name." What a beautiful thought—to become Love, and to act toward others with love and understanding at all times. Later, in Merton's book, *No Man Is an Island*, he added, "One thing that has suddenly hit me; that nothing counts except love."

The biblical passage in 1 Corinthians 13 connects Young's and Merton's words to Scripture:

> If I speak in the tongues of men and of angels, but have not love, I am only a resounding gong or a clanging symbol. If I have the

gift of prophecy and can fathom all mysteries and all knowledge, and if I have a faith that can move mountains, but have not love, I am nothing. If I give all I possess to the poor and surrender my body to the flames, but have not love, I gain nothing.

Love is patient, love is kind. It does not envy, it does not boast, it is not proud. It is not rude, it is not self-seeking, it is not easily angered, it keeps no record of wrongs. Love does not delight in evil but rejoices with the truth. It always protects, always trusts, always hopes, always perseveres.

Amen! These are the words Lu and I asked the ship's captain to read at our wedding in 2006. They are surely among the greatest words ever written.

Yes, the miracle given to me was all about "authentic love": the love I have for my wife Lu, my daughter Marni, my granddaughters Allison and Lucy, my family, my new extended family, and all of those who loved me through the good times and the bad. Certainly I love Black Sox, my special friend. And I will always love Chris and my stepchildren. I am sure they know that.

In early June, I was able to reflect during a return trip to Red Wing. On a cloudy Saturday morning, I sat on a wooden bench a few yards from the mighty Mississippi. Behind me the bustling sounds of a farmers' market interrupted the calm of the downtown streets.

In a few hours, I was to attend Allison's graduation party in a hundred-year-old barn northwest of the city. The previous evening, goose bumps traveled up and down my body as I sat beside my daughter Marni, and my granddaughter Lucy, and watched from a gymnasium row as my granddaughter Allison graduated from Red Wing High School. Clad in a beautiful purple robe with her blond hair flowing and a smile as big as the Grand Canyon spread across her face, Allison had completed twelve years of education, and was headed for Mary Baldwin College in Virginia. I had no doubt as I watched her receive her diploma that one day she would be a United States senator, or even president, a goal she only halfheartedly joked about.

After the ceremony, I delighted in watching Allison stand between her *three fathers*—yes, three: her birth father John, her adoptive father Rob, and her stepfather James. Each showed respect to the other despite any past differences. Seeing them together touched my heart, each loving Allison in a different way. When she stood on one side of me with Lucy on the other for a photo, my heart was beating a thousand miles an hour. I looked just like a thorn between two roses.

At the graduation party, I met more relatives from all sides of my new extended family, including Corky and Romayne, Rob's parents. Gifts from my two sisters and brother made Allison smile. I treasured the support from Anne, Jack, and Debbie, siblings who were embracing my miracle. Now Allison's uncles and aunts and friends from all around were also bringing presents, all in celebration of her achievement. Among them was Mary, Marni's adoptive mother, a lovely woman with a calming face. The previous evening she had told me she believed that her husband Gary, gone now but not forgotten, had "orchestrated" this whole thing, departing the earth so that Marni's birth father could appear. I had no doubt she was right, that his spirit was with us, that he was smiling along with my mom and dad in Heaven at the true miracle that had occurred.

Before I left Red Wing, Mary presented me with over twenty photographs of Marni. Many showed the love Marni and Gary shared. I must have looked at these photographs over a hundred times. I hoped Gary was watching from above knowing how grateful I was to him for loving Marni like he did.

As the party proceeded along, my throat became dry as I talked and talked some more with new people who were welcoming me into the family. Marni's husband James' parents Leon and Audrey, Rob's parents, and James' ex-wife Ann all embraced me and made me feel welcome. Leon, a weathered farmer with a lively step at seventy-five years old, explained how farmers can predict weather patterns and that "when the wind is from the northwest, all will be clear."

Watching Lucy interact with the adults and then play with her cousins gave me a real sense of pride. When I first saw her in Red Wing, she had given me a big hug and a nice peck on the cheek. I squeezed her tight and never wanted to let go. I felt goosebumps again when Marni let me know that Lucy wanted to be as close with me as Allison had been with Gary.

Throughout this unbelievable weekend, I was overwhelmed by how Marni orchestrated everything. She was the glue that had permitted John and his new wife Melissa; Rob; James and his ex-wife Ann, and their two children; and herself to interact respectfully among one another. Instead of having to choose sides, as had been the case with my divorce, Allison and Lucy felt love all around them from people who decided that love for their children came first. Not only had the Spirit brought me a daughter, but an astonishing one who called me "Dad" and expressed her love through e-mail and telephone calls almost every day.

Two weeks later, on Father's Day, with the Rocky Mountains luminous at the horizon, I sat on our apartment deck calmly reading the Sunday morning newspaper. Black Sox was playing in the living room with his ball after we had returned from an early morning hike along a nearby trail where a stream wove its way through the beautiful landscape. I thanked the Good Lord once again for my bountiful blessings. Marni had wanted to share our first Father's Day together, but she had called to tell me her father-in-law Leon had some health issues and she wasn't able to travel. She also explained what a good time she was having mowing the grass on Leon's farm as she "worked on her tan."

As nine o'clock on Father's Day rolled into view, I noticed Lu walking through the deck door with a Cheshire cat grin on her face. Instantly, I noticed that someone was behind her, and that someone was none other than my daughter Marni. And behind her was James, approaching with a light step. Marni hugged me tight and kissed me on the cheek while shouting, "Happy Father's Day!" In tears, *again*, I could not believe this wonderful gift, the gift of a daughter surprising her father, one she had only known existed for less than three months, one whom she once thought was dead.

During the hug, one that seemed to last forever, even Black Sox was startled at the sudden turn of events, wagging his tail in delight. Shocked, I sat down (before I fell down) still believing I was experiencing a dream instead of reality. In fact, on some days I was sure the whole experience was a dream, or at the very least, surreal.

Later, I would learn that Marni was not on Leon's farm the day before, but in nearby Estes Park. With Lu, James, and even my sisters Anne and Debbie as co-conspirators, the group had completely surprised me.

Throughout the day, we talked and laughed and laughed some more before sharing a special Father's Day dinner in downtown

Boulder. I was overwhelmed with elation. My eyes lit up when Marni gave me a black cardigan sweater of James' that I had admired, a pink tie, and a colorful card that said, "Happy Father's Day." These were my first Father's Day gifts, real Father's Day gifts, something I could never have imagined. Wearing the sweater made me feel close to James and Marni; it had been part of them and now it was part of me.

Two days after her surprise visit, Marni sent this e-mail:

Hi there Dad! What a wonderful time we had with you on Father's Day. Some wonderful memories. It was wonderful to see your face light up the way it did when you saw me come onto the patio . . . made me feel so loved. Know that you are . . . Marni

As I soaked in the loving words, I noticed that my daughter (I love saying that as many times a day as possible) had used the word "wonderful" three times. Yes, this was truly a wonderful gift, a wonderful blessing, a wonderful, unexpected miracle, and a wonderful Father's Day that I would never forget. The Spirit guiding me through the wondrous journey to discover Marni, Allison, and Lucy had bonded us forever.

EPILOGUE

When I told Marni and James about the two-hundred-page manuscript I wrote while Lu and I lived in Michigan chronicling the spiritual journey leading me to seminary and to marrying her, and that I had shelved it in anticipation of an ending of some sort, they were amazed. Recalling, and then recording, defining moments of my life materialized during a time when I was reflective, an important step toward becoming the contemplative person Thomas Merton advocates.

After connecting with Marni, I simply added the details of the miracle to what I had already written so I could recall the details as the months and years passed. While doing so, I was overwhelmed by the emotional responses received from family, friends and strangers amazed at the story of my miracle. Each was inspired in their own special way, each uniquely connected with some aspect of the miracle. One wrote of depression and how the story uplifted her; some shared their experiences with being adopted and then discovering their birth parents; and yet another, my Aspen friend Mike Hundert, told me of how the story made him treasure the true meaning of fatherhood. Some said the story made them laugh; others told me they cried. Many, including another Aspen friend, Paula Zurcher, told me I should share my life story with others.

Marni and James were touched after I told them of the heartwarming responses. When I mentioned the possibility of publishing a book that included the miracle, both, along with Allison and Lucy, embraced the idea with love and support.

I soon began updating the manuscript, a continuing process through the final months of 2010, as Lu and I continued to enjoy the blessings of our new extended family. In late November, we traveled once again to Red Wing to share the Thanksgiving holiday with our new families. Alongside us was Black Sox, who slept most of the trip as we made our way through Nebraska and Iowa to Minnesota. When we arrived, Lucy, her brown hair waving in the wind, scampered outside to greet me with a hug and a kiss on the cheek. Then I gave Marni, and then Allison, and then James big hugs as we stood in the kitchen. After a bit, Lucy and Allison sat on either side of me as I showed them photographs of members of my family, my parents, my grandparents, and even a great-grandparent or two. I also shared photographs of me as a six-month-old, growing up in Indiana wearing an odd green wool hat that made me look like a fool, and in college wearing a faded letter jacket with a *P* for Purdue on the front. When I pulled out yet another photograph, Lucy and Allison picked me out of a Little League All-Star team. Marni enjoyed two special photographs, one where I was seated next to James Stewart at the *Beverly Hills Christmas* taping, and the other interviewing actor Robert Duvall for my radio show.

To my delight, Marni told me she was writing some children's short stories about adoption, with a young girl named Luna as the main character. James was also writing, recounting his experiences while teaching a course of world religion that had landed him in trouble with the local clergy and school officials some years ago. That evening Lu and I enjoyed hearing Lucy sing in the children's choir at United Lutheran Church, the same church where Marni's adoptive father Gary not only was pastor but had also baptized Marni at six months old, and Lucy as an infant. And, of course, Lucy's singing voice was the best of them all.

During a Thanksgiving dinner overflowing with tasty dishes of fresh turkey, stuffing, mashed potatoes, gravy, corn, biscuits, and even my favorite, macaroni and cheese especially prepared for me, I glanced at son-in-law James, his daughter Kastina, his parents Audrey and Leon, and Rob, Lucy's father. Lucy was seated across from me and adjacent to Allison, home from college. On either side of me sat my favorite women, Lu and Marni.

After dinner, Lucy cuddled up next to me on the tan couch. I noticed she was wearing different-colored socks, a habit most friends teased me about, but something I now had in common with my very own granddaughter. Marni told me that even before meeting me, Lucy had worn the mismatched socks.

During the two months leading up to Christmas, my new vocabulary was in full swing. I used words and phrases such as, "What should we give our daughter for Christmas?" or "Do you think our granddaughter Lucy would like some new colored socks?" or "How about our granddaughter Allison? Shouldn't we find a special book for her about politics since this is her interest right now?" These new questions, ones never contemplated nine months earlier, were suddenly of great importance.

One sunny day while walking Black Sox through the neighboring mountain trails, I realized that since my spiritual transformation my mind was now filled with thoughts impossible before and during the Bob Knight war. This caused me to recall once again James Allen's words in *What Man Thinketh*, that we are what we think. Through the lessons of my teachers, among others, James and Job in the Bible, Pastor Rick Warren, Pastor Charles Stanley, Thomas

Merton, and Lao-tzu, I had incorporated an entirely new thought process. I loved this spiritual makeover and my new self, how I was thinking good Christlike thoughts from morning until night.

Yes, my mind was fresh, alive with thoughts of how to help people, how to be the type of lay minister I wanted to be with everyone with whom I interacted. I found it difficult to explain this new mindset to others, to employ words to convey my feelings. There was a glow about me now, an inner emotion of joy, of happiness. When I told Lu about it one evening, she relayed how this sort of "feeling" was akin to the teachings of Buddhism in that the thoughts we have are also karma and have karmic effects. Certainly the new mindset had propelled countless blessings as I evolved into the new Mark Shaw, one noted by Merton in *New Seeds of Contemplation* when he described how transformation emerges on a "gradual basis," not all at once. For me, "gradual" had meant many years of renewal; many years of learning, of changing everything about what I had been to become what I believed was now a decent human being.

One morning Lu and I began talking about Christmas presents. At first I thought she suggested we give the new family a "card," but she corrected me to say "car." My face lit up at the great idea, and better still, I told her we should surprise Marni, James and the girls with the Christmas gift we knew they needed. They had accumulated many miles on their car, and we had a spare, a black Nissan Versa that we really did not use anymore. After some quick planning, by mid-morning of the twenty-third of December, we were standing outside a car wash in Red Wing ready to spring our surprise on Marni just as she had surprised me with her Father's Day visit.

With similar intentions, I called Marni from the car wash and said, "Okay, we are at the Denver airport. It is really busy and the security is going to take some time but everyone is in the holiday spirit" and so forth. She asked whether we had been through the new body screening security devices, and what time we would land in Minnesota. All the while, I had to keep from snickering since we were now less than five minutes from her house.

After we parked the Versa with a huge red bow on its hood in Marni's driveway, Lu rang the back doorbell. Within a few seconds, there was Marni looking out at us with amazement. "What are you doing here?" she asked. "I thought . . . " she stammered as we shouted, "Surprise!"

Marni walked toward us. Two big hugs later, I noticed a tear in her eye. She discovered the car while I said, "Here, read this" and handed her our holiday card. She opened it and began reading the poem I had written for her. She was still confused over the surprise of our appearance when she thought we were still in Denver. Lu presented her with the keys, and with James now at her side, Marni walked to the Versa with a stunned look on her face and examined the inside. Tears rolled down her cheeks as I watched with a father's love. When Marni hugged Lu and me again, she would not let go.

During an evening service in which Lucy sang again with her church choir, Marni passed a small note back to me. At the top of the paper was typed "Kid's Notes," and below it she had written, "Like a glow worm," a reference, as she explained to me earlier, to the times when Marni, as a child, had felt darkness all around her. And that now, finally having the love of her birth parents, she felt like the old battery-powered "glow worm" toy that provided her guidance and light. But it was the handwritten word "Dad" on the front of the note that hit me the hardest. Reading that word made me want to jump up and shout for the entire church congregation to hear: "Like Mary and Joseph who were about to be parents to a son, Jesus, I have a child as well. Like them, I have been given the greatest gift of all, one brought to me by the Holy Spirit." A little dramatic, I knew, so I just kept my mouth shut and stayed put.

On Christmas Eve, Lu and I enjoyed the love of our new families through a memorable dinner at James' parents' farm. After enjoying a feast that once again included macaroni and cheese, Leon told stories like *Rudolph the Red-nosed Reindeer* to those gathered around him. Then we sang traditional Christmas songs. The next morning I saw once again the blessings of fatherhood when our new family opened their presents. I watched Lucy discover a telescope, Allison open a Marilyn Monroe memorabilia book, James laugh as he tried on a black Chinese jacket with a gold dragon emblazoned on the front, Marni turning the pages of a book called *Sauces* that was six inches thick, and Rob enjoying a wooden tie and a puzzle featuring the fifty-three "Fourteeners" (fourteen-thousand-foot peaks) in Colorado. Lu was surprised by her nifty polka-dotted rubber boots (Wellies, as Marni calls them), great for our Colorado winters. She and I laughed when we opened a box with a GPS receiver in it, as we were often referred to as "Mr. and Mrs. Lost." We were terrible at directions and usually ended up lost on some road heading for nowhere. Lu and I reveled at our present of a handmade 2011 calendar featuring photographs of Marni, Allison, Lucy, Lu and me.

Everyone laughed and had fun, and later in the day, Marni and Lu coaxed me into singing my silly and bad rendition of Roy Orbison's song, *Runnin' Scared*. Lu laughed so hard she was crying, and Lucy and Allison giggled, wondering who this crazy grandfather of theirs really was. When Lucy emulated the "huh, huh, huh, huh—huh, huh, huh, huh" verse that I had butchered while peeking around the kitchen door, we all screamed. To be certain, love was everywhere on this once-in-a-lifetime first Christmas.

In *New Seeds of Contemplation*, Merton said, "Love is our true destiny." Philosopher Reinhold Niebuhr echoed this truth with his words, "Nothing we do, however virtuous, can be accomplished alone; therefore we are saved by love. No virtuous act is quite as virtuous from the standpoint of our friend or foe as it is from our standpoint. Therefore, we must be saved by the final form of love, which is forgiveness."

Love and forgiveness—the twin pillars of true joy in our lives. I now understood that learning how to love and how to forgive was my true destiny. By looking in the mirror and critically analyzing my reflection, I could accept myself and my actions, and move on. Life now wasn't just about me—as all parents know, it was about giving. Fatherhood had taught me about selflessness and generosity.

God graced me with love in every aspect of my life, from my wife Lu, from my new daughter and granddaughters, from my new family, from my immediate family, from my special friends, and from Black Sox. Without doubt, I am truly the most blessed man on the face of the earth because, through my transformation, I have learned not only how to love and forgive myself, but also how to love and forgive others. Thomas Merton wrote that the real question in life is not whether one "is happy but whether one is free." By traveling on my spiritual road to a miracle, I now am.

The Shaw Family – Marvin, Vera (Back Row), Mark, Jack, Anne
(Front Row) – ca. 1948

Mark and his parents on Purdue Graduation Day – 1968

Mark covering the famous Calaveras County (CA) Frog Jumping Contest
for ABC's *Good Morning America* – 1978

James Stewart, Mark, and Burt Reynolds at the taping of
A Beverly Hills Christmas with James Stewart – 1987

Mark at a booksigning for *Larry Legend*, a biography of Larry Bird – 1999

Mark on the radio with "Mr. Hollywood" in Bloomington, IN
before the Knightmare – 2000

Mark with brother Jack, and sisters Anne and Debbie – 2003

Mark, Lu, and Black Sox on the couple's wedding day – July 2006

At age sixty-two, Mark's San Francisco Theological Seminary
graduation day – 2008

To see if Marni and Mark's facial features matched, her husband
James pasted two photographs together – March 2010

Marni and her adoptive family – Mary and Gary (seated),
and Marcus, Erik, Marni and Paul – January 2008

Marni and Mark's first photograph as father/daughter –
Eldorado Canyon State Park, CO – April 2010

Marni surprises Mark for Father's Day 2010

Mark and granddaughters Allison and Lucy atop
Vail Mountain – July 2010

Mark's first Christmas with the new family – James, Allison, Rob, Lucy, Marni, Mark, and Kastina – 2010

James, Lu, Mark, Marni, Allison, and Lucy – Boulder, CO – Easter 2011

ACKNOWLEDGMENTS

Thanking all of those who are responsible for the miracle in my life, and this book, would add another ten pages to the text. But gratitude has to begin with my wife Wen-ying Lu, the shining light in my life. Her embracing my daughter and two grandchildren is just one indication of her loving ways.

Certainly special thanks go to James Morrison, Marni's husband, for locating me so that I might experience this miracle. I also thank Marni, Allison and Lucy for accepting into their lives this crazy guy who turned out to be their father and grandfather. Every time I think about them I smile.

In the film *Forrest Gump*, the Tom Hanks character says, "My momma always said life was like a box of chocolates. You never know what you're gonna get." What did Lu and I get with our new family? Terrific people all around. I thank Mary and Gary Peterson who brought Marni into their lives and raised such a wonderful daughter, and Paul, Erik, and Marcus Peterson and their families for loving this whirlwind daughter of mine. Rob Fuglestad deserves a heartfelt thank you for being a great father to both Allison and Lucy and a great friend to me. To Leon and Audrey Morrison, Corky and Romayne Fuglestad, and all those in my new extended family, I say thank you for treating Lu and me with such kindness and love. To Marni's birth mother, I say thank you again for your courage to give birth to our daughter Marni, a gift that has brought us so much happiness and joy.

To my own immediate family, including brother Jack and his wife Sue, sister Anne and sister Debbie and her husband David, thanks for always being there for me. And for understanding how much discovering a daughter and two grandchildren has been such a true blessing.

To friends Pete and Alice Dye, Scott and Janice Montross, Hugh and Pearl Campion, Diane Darsch, Becky Miller, Becky Jones, Jerry and Pat Bales, Bob Haverstick, and gifted editor Kristina Howard, thank you for your comments and suggestions through your reading of manuscript drafts. To my daughter Marni, who is a terrific editor as well, thank you for helping make this book so much better through your comments and suggestions. To Patrick Hasburgh, I thank you for your friendship and for writing the book's foreword. To Pete and Alice Dye, Squire Rushnell, Don Lattin, Dr. Lewis Rambo, David Brofsky, Rev. Jim Burklo, and Dr. Paul Pearson, thank you for writing endorsements for the book. I also thank journalist Erika Meltzer for her article about the miracle in the *Boulder Daily Camera*.

Through the years so many people have been great friends and supporters and I thank them for their caring ways. They include, among others, Sheri and Mitch Spahn, Jack Leer, Jack Lupton, Pete and Alice Dye and their assistants Dinky and Shannon, Bob Haverstick, Bobby and Leslie Weed, Koren Reyes, Mike and Anne Horii, Pearl and Hugh Campion, Scott and Janice Montross, Judy Deputy, Paula Zurcher, Richie Cummins and his assistant Allison, Dave Danforth, Mike, Carol, Danny and Kevin Hundert, Woody Fraser and Cathy Masamitsu, Al Arens, Dave and Nancy Foley, Pat Riley, Mary Beth Ramey, Jerry and Pat Bales, Becky Miller, Becky Jones, Mike Stipher and Joanie Green, Becky Howard, Ken Birkemeier, Rudy Crabtree, Dave Gonzenbach, Debbie Hayes and her mother Audrey, Betsy Blankenbaker, Tom Yoder, Gary and Sally Boone, Don and Corrine Larsen, Tom Day, Jesse and Aundrina, Susie McSweeney,

Robert and Iza Peszek, San Francisco Theological Seminary professors Lewis Rambo, Bob and Polly Coote, Elizabeth Liebert, Christopher Ocker, Eung-Chun Park, and Herman Waetjen, my fellow SFTS classmates including Clarita, Doug, and Don, and Lu's Michigan State University and University of Colorado at Boulder colleagues and friends, and Pastor Peter Terpenning.

At People's Press, I thank Mirte Mallory, the tireless publisher whose wisdom impressed me the moment I first spoke with her; Nicole Beinstein Strait, a gifted writer and editor whose novels will be published in the future; George Stranahan, a true visionary; and Catherine Lutz, a line editor extraordinaire. Also thank you to the folks at Globe Pequot Press for their support of the book, and to Nick Zelinger for his creativity in designing the cover.

Without doubt, Black Sox the wonder dog has been a supportive influence every single day since he entered my life in 2003. At five a.m., he pokes his nose into my sleepy face as if to say, "Okay, Mark, start writing."

Above all, I thank the Holy Spirit for guiding me through an incredible spiritual journey culminating in the discovery of Marni, Allison and Lucy. Hopefully this story will inspire others to believe in miracles, to believe that anything, *anything at all*, is possible.

— Mark Shaw

DISCUSSION QUESTIONS

1. What is a miracle? Do you believe in miracles; why or why not? Are miracles spiritual in nature? Where do they come from?

2. Mark Shaw writes that one must be open to receiving a miracle, and that he was being "prepared" for his miracle all his life. What kind of miracles have you experienced in your life? What experiences do you know of where others have enjoyed miracles in their lives? Are you expecting a miracle in your life?

3. Mark's life is like one giant road trip. How do you feel about people who keep traveling down different roads trying to find themselves and their true purpose in life?

4. Fame is such a strong aphrodisiac. Do you know of instances in which fame has caused people problems? Do you think Mark was too caught up with his experiences with celebrities and Hollywood, or was he just having fun? Do you think there are real differences between people in America who live on the coasts compared to those who live in the Midwest or in the mountains, as Mark suggests?

5. How do you think Mark Shaw and Bob Knight each handled the incident that led to Knight's firing and Mark's separation rom his wife and stepchildren? Is Mark right that he put his own interests ahead of his stepchildren's well-being or is he being too hard on himself?

6. Mark considers the incident with Bob Knight as having been meant to be. Do you believe in coincidences, fate or destiny? Are they one in the same? Does every event in one's life have meaning, or just a few? Can you only fulfill your destiny by being conscious of your decisions and actions?

7. Pastor Rick Warren writes in *The Purpose Driven Life* that we must forgive those who hurt us; otherwise we carry the burden of anger or hatred around with us. If this is true, does forgiveness also mean forgetting, and/or reengaging with those who have hurt us?

8. Pastor Warren also suggests that to mend a broken relationship, we should apologize even if we don't feel we did anything wrong. Is this a moral or ethical thing to do? Who truly benefits from this behavior?

9. What does it mean to truly love one another, and why do many people believe that love is the only thing in the world that matters? Is this practical, and is it possible to live in the material world with only love as your guide?

10. Do you think it is truly possible to divorce civilly, and if there are children involved, for the parents to remain friends and co-parent effectively? When should parents' feelings come before their children's?

11. Do you believe that Mark always wanted to have his own biological children? If he did, why did he not make his wish a priority? Was becoming a biological father through a loving marriage ever in his control? If Mark had never learned of Marni's existence, do you think his life could have been fulfilled through his marriage to Lu, his friendships, his role as a Big Brother and coach to other people's children, and through his professional work?

12. Both Mark and his wife Lu fully embraced Marni and her family into their lives. Would you have done the same? Why do you think Lu in particular was able to accept her role as stepmother so graciously?

13. At times Marni wondered if she might be returned to the adoption agency if she was "bad." She also felt "incomplete" before meeting her birth parents. Do these feelings surprise you?

14. What effects do parenting styles have on children's upbringings and personalities? How significant a role can a stepparent or adoptive parent play in a child's life, and can they make up for any loss of a biological parent?

15. Mark wrote that "Religion answers questions; spirituality questions answers." What does this mean? Can you be religious and not spiritual, or spiritual and not religious, or be both religious and spiritual simultaneously?

16. Thomas Merton wrote that we must let our old selves "die" before we can change and "live" again. Is this a gradual process, or something that happens through a specific event, or both? Have you ever felt that you have been changing inside over a long period of time, but others have only noticed your transformation much later on? Is our transformation ever truly finished?